HARDPRESS.NET
HOME OF HARD-TO-FIND BOOKS

Bees, Pigeons, Rabbits, and the Canary Bird,
Familiarly Described
by Peter Boswell

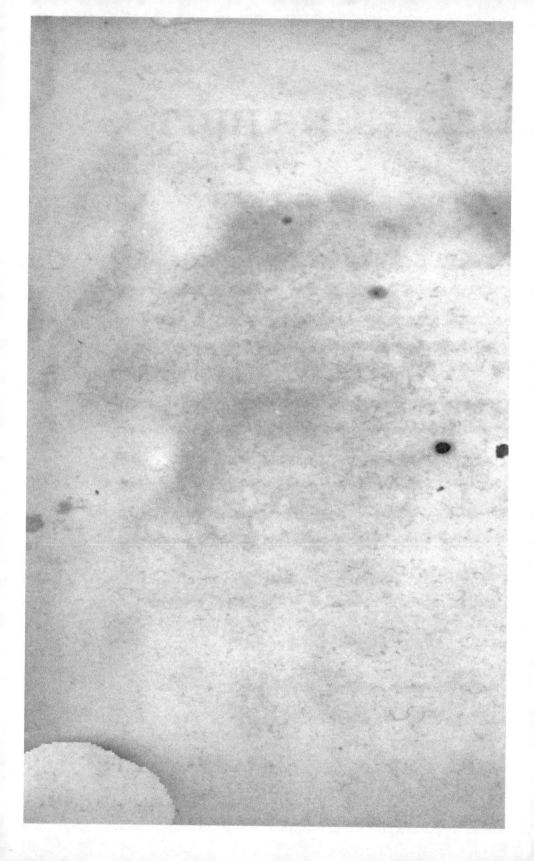

BEES, PIGEONS, RABBITS,

AND

THE CANARY BIRD,

FAMILIARLY DESCRIBED:

THEIR HABITS, PROPENSITIES, AND DISPOSITIONS EXPLAINED;
MODE OF TREATMENT IN HEALTH AND DISEASE PLAINLY
LAID DOWN; AND THE WHOLE ADAPTED AS A
TEXT-BOOK FOR THE YOUNG STUDENT.

BY PETER BOSWELL, OF GREENLAW.

•———

WITH AN APPENDIX,

CONTAINING DIRECTIONS FOR THE CARE OF SEVERAL

AMERICAN SINGING-BIRDS.

———

NEW-YORK:
WILEY AND PUTNAM.
1842.

TO THE READER.

In rearing or breeding the Canary, the Bee, the Pigeon, or Rabbit, no failure can take place if attention is paid to the regulations we have herewith recorded. Experience is perhaps the best school in which practical knowledge is obtained. This was the academy in which we ourselves were taught. To another school we have now endeavoured to introduce our youthful readers, where, by leaving the theory, we hope to have given them a light to guide them in the gratification of their innocent and favourite amusements.

THE AUTHOR.

Greenlaw, 1842.

J. P. WRIGHT, Printer, 18 New Street, New York.

APPENDIX.

AMERICAN MOCKING-BIRD.

The Mocking Bird, so justly celebrated for its vocal powers, is a native of America, and esteemed by every one who once hears him. Of himself he is all, breathing forth a concert of hundreds, of grove and field, shaming the originals into silence. At daylight, mid-day, and the live-long summer's night, his unceasing exertions demand applause. $150 we have known to be refused for a favourite bird, so docile as to come at a whistle, perch on his owner's hand and head, and while there to warble incessantly.

" The treatment of the Mocking Bird is not very peculiar or troublesome, requiring to be regularly fed every morning with Indian meal mixed among milk to a not very stiff paste. During the season of whortleberries, they should be allowed a plentiful supply in a small saucer; the same of cedar, elder, and poke-b rries, and wild cherries, in the months of October and November; as these birds will never thrive without a great deal of natural food. An egg boiled hard and grated is very good occasionally; a small piece of raw minced beef is also of service; during the summer season air is of benefit, but not in the sun; a little water in a cup for washing, once a day, is of service; but the greatest care is required when they are moulting, which commences early in August, and continues till November; then your bird should be kept quiet, and away from cold draughts of air, which are very injurious. During the moulting season, supply your bird plentifully with berries, *spiders* and *grasshoppers*, which are essential, especially the former, as in their native woods they live mainly on insects. It is of importance your bird is fed and watered *regularly every morning* by eight o'clock; for if fed one day early, another day late, and another day forgot, your bird will lose his spirit, and finally pine away.

" When this bird becomes sickly, it is necessary to treat him very kindly ; give him spiders daily, also *meal worms*, which can be had in granaries ; and suffer as little disturbance as possible ; also put gravel on the bottom of the cage.

" The male is known from the female by a regular line of white feathers in the wing, which in a fine bird forms almost a regular curve from the shoulder to the tip of the wing. They are, however, after all, difficult to distinguish, as some of the finest birds, when young, have been irregularly marked ; they are not completely plumed until they are two years old."

THE ROBIN.

Another favourite native of America, equally esteemed for its richness of song and delicacy of taste. A sprightly and beautiful bird. The plumage of the male is of a dark ashy grey, the head and tail black, with the breast of a bright mahogany red, the throat barred with white and black, and the eye of a piercing hazel, surrounded with a ring of white.

Their treatment is precisely the same as the Mocking Bird, and in confinement their docility is surprising, coming in and out of the house, and following their owner, and may even be taught to repeat small pieces of music. Birds have been taught to whistle psalm tunes, as dull as OLD HUNDRED, with methodistical precision, and in confinement they possess a talent for mimicry, and readily acquire the pronunciation of distinct words. Some have been known to whistle tunes with such accuracy, that even eyes and ears were found necessary to convince the listener that it was not a flute.

THE INDIGO BIRD.

The Indigo Bird is a native of America of surpassing beauty. Its song is lively, unique and interesting, and given not only at early dawn, but during the intense heat of mid-day in summer, and again is frequently heard during a great part of the night, especially if it be moonlight. Its notes resemble those of the Canary, and it may be kept in confinement on precisely the same food as given to the adult birds of that species. The male of this species is a brilliant azure blue with a reflection of green, the female of a dingy yellow and olive brown, rather inclined to purple. It is sometimes called the Blue Linnet, though in every way a distinct species from the true American Linnet or Purple Finch (Fringilla Purpurea). During the spring season they may be given occasionally insects, and they are particularly fond of the leaves or tops of the common garden beet. They are frequently sold in our markets in the months of May and June, and are very social and delightful songsters.

THE AMERICAN YELLOW-BIRD.

A beautiful and constant resident, dreading neither the severity of winter nor the heat of summer, always cheerful and light-hearted; it flies from field to field in company with its jocund companions; it seems a fit emblem of happiness, when, on the wing, as it moves in continued rises and falls, its notes of conversation are ever heard, and while setting on some lowly thistle or devoted lettuce stock, it converses occasionally with low liquid voice to its more humble and less noticed mate. No bird is more familiar, and but for its destruction of house and garden seeds, would be a universal favourite.

When trapped, they soon become familiar in the cage, and their music rivals the sonorous whistle of the canary, and is scarcely surpassed by it. They at times gradually elevate and lower their notes in the most delightful manner; bursting in an instant into overpowering melody, then dying away in a fairy-like strain, until it seems lost in the distance, then reviving with redoubled strength, running at once into the loudest fife of the Canary. They are very hardy and will bear considerable cold. Every sunny day should see their cage hung out, as air and sun-light are necessary to the health of this delightful bird; a saucer of water should be kept constantly in the cage, which should be well gravelled, as he is particularly fond of bathing. They are fond of rich and oily seeds, and should be reared on yellow canary, millet and hemp, 1½ of the latter; a little sunflower and lettuce seeds occasionally given them would be quite an addition to their fare. They are very fond of the leaves of the garden beet and salad, which should be occasionally fed to them, Apple should be given occasionally. The male is of a brilliant chrome yellow, with the crown of the head, wings and tail glossy black, the two latter edged with white, the female is of a dark colour, and may readily be distinguished.

THE PURPLE FINCH, OR LINNET.

A native bird of considerable pretensions to musical skill; in truth a delightful songster, very far superior to the Canary. They winter in Pennsylvania, and about the 1st of May retire to the North to breed. They fly in vast flocks, and are taken in trap cages, and sold at high prices under the name of *Linnets.* They very soon become familiar, but sometimes refuse to sing in confinement. From an excellent work on Ornithology, we copy the following notice of their musical powers; and in no way does it exceed the reality.

"The song of this beautiful *Finch* is, indeed, much finer than that of the Canary, the notes are remarkably clear and mellow, and the trilling sweet and various, particularly on their first arrival. At times the warble is scarcely audible, and appears at a distance; it then by a fine crescendo bursts into loudness, and falls into an ecstacy of ardent and overpowering expression: at such times the usual pauses of the song are forgotten, and like the varied lay of the Nightingale, the ravishing performer, as if in serious emulation, seems to study every art to produce the effect of *brilliant* and well contrasted harmony. The rapidity of his performance, and the prominent execution with which it is delivered, seem almost like the effort of a musical box, or fine-toned quietly-moving delicate strain of the organ."

Canary, hemp, millet and sunflower seeds may be fed to them; of the latter they are very fond. Juniper and cedar berries should be given them occasionally through the winter; salad and beet tops also, during the summer.

CONTENTS.

THE BEE.

THE PIGEON.

THE RABBIT.

THE CANARY BIRD.

APPENDIX.

THE BEE.

1. *Natural History of the Bee.*—Providence, that delights in spreading beneficence as well as beauty over all creation, has wisely formed the bee as an humble but active and untiring agent, in gathering up for the most important purposes, and converting to the most valuable use, the scraps and fragments of nature which would otherwise be scattered by the "viewless winds," and spread through the "ambient air." She has adorned the song of the poet, pointed the tale of the moralist, and furnished food to the hungry in the desert. Virgil calls the bee a ray of the divinity; Plutarch pronounced her a magazine of virtues; Quintilian asserts that she is the greatest of geometricians; and Watts, by calling in poetry to the aid of morality, has rendered her figure the means of interest, improvement, and delight to many a youthful mind. Philosophy has stooped to examine her habits and to watch over her haunts; she has presented the models of science and called forth the attention of scientific men; by her the husbandman has been cheered when sitting in his cottage garden, in his evening reflections on his day of

2

toil ; and in whatever light she may be viewed, there is none who can declare that he has no interest in her ways.

The bee, or honey-fly, according to naturalists, belongs to the fourth order of insects, and has four wings—the community or hive containing three kinds, namely, the queen, or mother-bee, the drone, and the working-bee.

To the queen, or mother of the whole community, it is necessary for the bee-master to give the strict. est attention, as, without a queen, it is useless to possess a hive, since neither can the generation of fresh swarms proceed, nor will those which may be present, labour, but will either emigrate, languish or die. The queen-bee is to be distinguished from the others by her colour and her size. She is larger and more tapering in her body. She is armed with a sting, which she, however, seldom uses energetically, either as the sceptre of her sovereignty, or the sword of her power. In the hive she reigns supreme, per. mitting no rival near her throne. Since the creation of her race, no prince-consort has to the queen.bee been known. By infallible instinct she is followed by the whole hive ; and where she is not, none will long remain. Her wings being shorter than those of the other bees, she flies more slowly, and can therefore be followed with less difficulty. Although she has been known to live for five or six years, she may never have occasion to use her wings all that time.

Mr. HUISH, a most able, practical, and comprehen. sive writer on the subject, says :

" The form of the Queen is wholly different from that of other bees. Like the drones, she neither has nor needs the triangular store cavities in her hinder thighs: her teeth are smaller than those of the working-bee, but larger than those of the drone, and she has no bunches of hair or bristle near her feet; she is longer in her body, and more tapering than the drone. Her belly is of a golden colour, and the upper part of her is of a brighter hue than that of the common bee. But the most unerring rule to judge of the queen-bee is from the shortness of her wings, which extend only to the third ring of her body, whilst those of the working-bees, and more particularly those of the drones, cover almost their whole length. Thus she flies with greater difficulty than the working-bees; however, it is mere accident, if, in the course of her life, she should have any occasion for her wings."

By some peculiar process of impregnation she becomes the mother of the whole colony, laying the eggs which are fecundated by the drones, and from which all the rest proceed, whether they be future queens, drones, or workers. Her fruitfulness, from whatever cause insecto-anatomists may conceive it to arise, almost exceeds belief; for she continues to deposit eggs as long as a single cell remains vacant to receive them. She might, therefore, with more truth be styled the mother, rather than the queen of the bees, as, at the present moment, it is the earnest prayer of every loyal Briton that the terms in a higher quarter may be speedily conjoined. The queen soon pines and dies without her subjects, and they

immediately cease to labour when separated from
their queen. To compensate for death, accident, or
incapacity, preparations are immediately made for
the formation of a new royal personage ; and at the
proper season young queens are to be found at every
stage of progress. The successor is formed from the
larva of the common bee, which is supplied with
royal food, not in the common hexagonal cells, but
in one of a peculiar construction—an oblong sphe-
roid—and of a larger size. The young princesses,
varying in number from five to six dozens, reach maturity about the sixteenth day, and those of them that
are not required are thrown out of the hive. On this
subject the remarks of Mowbray are judicious, and
contain almost all that the young apiarian requires.
He says, "The cells both of the drones and the
working-bees are horizontal. The cell of the drone
is of an irregular form, that of the working or common bee a perfect hexagon. On the side of the middle combs the cell is constructed, which is destined
to receive the egg of which a young queen is to be
born. It has been discovered by the curious that
nature imparts the wonderful faculty to the queen of
foreknowing the kind of egg she is about to lay, and
of choosing the particular cell in which it ought to
be placed. Such are the discoveries or opinions of
practical Apiarians.

Should the number of labouring bees be insuffi-
cient for the purpose of constructing the necessary
cells, the queen will most probably forsake the hive,
however well supplied with provision, and will be
most ready to take this step in fine weather. All, or

part of the stock, will follow, assisting her, it is averred, when wearied, from being unaccustomed to flight, by bearing her up with their legs and wings. The old remedy to prevent this desertion, was to place empty combs in the hive, which does not always succeed, from the disgust taken by the queen. The preferable method is supposed to be, when there is a hive at hand, the colony of which has died through the season, to place over it the hive about to be deserted. The eggs left in the borrowed hive will thus be hatched, and a colony raised in sufficient numbers. The accidental death of the queen, or departure, will occasion the bees to forsake their hive. Some years since, according to report, the Rev. Dr. Dunbar, by a series of experiments in Scotland, ascertained that when a queen-bee is wanting in a hive, she may be produced from the egg of a working-bee. In one experiment, the queen being removed, the bees set about constructing royal cells, and placing common *larvæ* in them : in seven days two queens were formed. One of these killed the other, and though, while in a virgin state, the surviving queen was treated by the bees with no distinction whatever, she no sooner began to lay, than she became the object of constant solicitude and respect by her admiring subjects, who watched, fed, and waited upon her.

The common or working bees are the smallest in size, and, in a good swarm, are computed to amount to from twelve to twenty thousand in number. For a long time the principal or queen-bee was supposed to be a male, and was called the king, which modern research has discovered to be female; and by the same means it has been proved that the working bees are of the same gender in an undeveloped form.

The cells in which the workers' eggs are deposited lie in the centre of the hive: they are there first deposited by the queen, and are in size such as those produced by the butterfly. They are hatched in four or five days: for four or six days more they remain in the larva or grub state, during which period they are tended and fed by the nurse bees. The nymph or pupa form is then assumed: they next wind themselves into a cocoon or film, and the nurse bees carefully enclose them with wax. The perfect bee bursts forth from its imprisonment on the twenty-first day from the laying of the egg. It is quickly cleaned by its companions, and in a few hours may be seen gathering honey "from every opening flower" in the garden or field around its hive.

"In examining the STRUCTURE of the common working-bee," says Buffon, "the first remarkable part that offers is the trunk (*proboscis*), which serves to extract the honey from flowers. It is not formed like that of other flies, in the manner of a tube, through which the fluid is to be sucked up, but like a besom to sweep, or tongue to lick it up. The insect is also furnished with teeth, enabling it to work upon materials collected, the *pollen* and *farina* of flowers, from an elaboration of which, in the stomach of the bee, are to be derived both the honey and wax. In the thighs of the hinder legs are found two cavities, fringed with hair, and into these, as into a basket, the bee deposits the pellets it has collected. Thus employed, it flies from flower to flower, increasing its stores, until the pellet or ball upon each thigh acquires the size of a grain of pepper; when having obtained a sufficient load, it returns homewards, making the best way to the hive."

The belly of the bee is divided into six rings, which, by slipping one over the other, shorten the dimensions of the body. Pliny held that the body of the bee is furnished with pores, through which the animal breathes; and to this opinion, Lisle, the agricultural writer, has assented. The contents of the insect's belly, besides the common intestines, are the honey-bag, the venom-bag, and the sting. The honey-bag is transparent as crystal, containing the honey which has been collected—the greater part of which is deposited in the hive, being passed into the cells of the honey-combs, whilst the remainder serves for the insect's nourishment, as, during the summer or labouring season, it never touches the store laid by for winter.

The sting, which serves to defend this little animal from its enemies, is composed of three parts, the sheath and two darts, which are extremely small and penetrating. These darts have several small points or barbs, like those of a fish-hook, which render the sting more painful, the darts rankling in the wound. Still, however, the infliction from such an instrument would be very slight, had not the bee power to poison the wound. The sheath, which has a sharp point, makes the first impression; the darts act next; after which the venomous fluid is infused. The sheath sometimes, urged perhaps by the degree of excitement in the insect, sticks so fast in the wound, that it is left behind, and causes more permanent inflammation. The bee, in consequence, soon after dies, from an eruption of the intestines.

It might, on first consideration, appear well for mankind if the bee had not the power of inflicting such wounds; but, on farther reflection, it will be found that the little animal would have too many rivals in sharing the profits of its labours. Numerous other animals, fond of honey, and of obtaining it at free cost, would intrude upon the sweets of the hive without armed guardians for its protection. The venom of the insects appears to be an original material in their composition, imparted to them by nature for defence or revenge, and not formed, like honey, from ingredients collected externally.

Among the working bees there is a complete division of labour—some being employed in secreting and spreading wax, and constructing cells; others, in warming the eggs, guarding the queen, and giving warning of external danger; while the rest ransack the fields, flying from flower to flower in search of honey or farina, loaded with which they fly homeward to the hive. There is great difference of opinion regarding the length of life in working-bees, but it is generally believed that they are short-lived, and that their place is speedily supplied.

It is computed that the drones, or male bees, are half the number of the other bees in every swarm. They are stingless; in size, between the queen and common bee, and may be distinguished by their loud and peculiar hum. The cells in which the eggs, from which they spring, are laid, are larger than those of the common bees, stronger, and nearer the side of the hive. Twenty-five or twenty-six days is the period in which they pass through their various stages. Their life extends from April to August or September, at which time they are indiscriminately massacred by the working-bees. The drone is full at the extremity or tail, which the wings cover, excepting a small angle which has a blackish appearance. Beneath are two small protuberances, which are the supposed indications of the masculine gender. The drone is left by nature unarmed, the organs of generation in him being found in the place of the sting in the working-bee. The *antennæ* and *proboscis* of the drones are shorter than those of the labouring bees, and their teeth smaller; nor have they those cavities on the thighs which distinguish the latter, their sole destined employment being the propagation of their kind, for which they are furnished with food from the common stock, towards the collection of which they never give, nor are expected to give, any assistance.

The drone has been a much slandered creature,—but the great Author of nature has done nothing in vain; and it clearly appears that the drone serves a most important purpose in the economy of the hive. It has been supposed by some that the drones fecundate the eggs deposited by the queen; but this cannot be, for the greater number of these are laid and hatched after the drones are destroyed, and before a new race of them are brought forth in the spring. The truth is, the eggs are rendered productive by the drones before they are deposited by the queen; and when this has been done, she remains fruitful as long as she lives, and has no need of drones for the only purpose they were designed to serve. If a hive, according to Bonner and Huber, is forcibly deprived of its young queen, no expulsion or destruction of the drones takes place; the purposes of their nature not having been yet accomplished. They are retained, in case of need, for the production of other queens, whose eggs they must render fruitful. In ventilating hives, where swarming is unnecessary, on account of abundance of space, the young queens themselves are expelled, followed by the destruction of the drones at an earlier period than, in other circumstances, it would have occurred. They are then useless, and their expulsion often takes place as early as May; but in the common swarming hives, as new queens may still require to be fecundated, to form the heads of new clans, the onslaught does not take place till July or August. All this distinctly proves that the purpose served by the drones is to render the queen's eggs productive. If this object is not required, they are sacrificed, but if it is, they are spared. They are not allowed to remain a burden on the common stock, when they can be of no farther use, and the destruction of the drones may be considered as a safe and sure indication that no farther swarming is contemplated. Dr. Bevan, in his work entitled the "Honey Bee," observes, "that the number of drones may be considered as in accordance, in some degree, with the general profuseness of nature; we find her abounding with supernumeraries in a great variety of instances, in the blossoms of trees, and flowers, as well as in the relative number of one sex to another among animals." Huber conceives that it was necessary there should be a great number of drones, that the queen might be sure of finding one in her excursion through the expanse of the atmosphere, and run no risk of sterility.

2. *Swarming.*—In the generality of cases, swarming with bees is an act of necessity. If required, it can easily be prevented by the enlargement or ventilation of the hive. A crowded population and an increasing temperature lead the bee to seek relief by emigration, just as we ourselves pant after the fresh breeze when confined to the stifling atmosphere of the theatre or the ball-room. Mr. Huber says, " We have frequently proved the heat of the hive by the thermometer. In a populous hive the heat continues of nearly one temperature, until the tumult which precedes swarming, which increases the heat to such a degree as to be intolerable to the bees. When exposed to it, they rush impetuously towards the outlet of the hive and depart." Kirby and Spence say, " Bees being confined to a given space, which they possess not the means of enlarging,—to avoid the ill effects of being too much crowded, when their population exceeds a certain limit, they must necessarily emigrate."

When there is a first swarm, the new colony is generally led forth by the old queen, who leaves the heir to her throne behind in an embryo state. In the majority of cases an equal number of young and

old bees, with a few hundreds of drones, form the
swarm.

Many from vanity, and some from ignorance, are
disposed to boast of the number of swarms they can
extract from each hive in the course of a single season, but this is a foolish idea, and often a fatal mistake. By this practice we may certainly increase
the number of hives in the Apiary, but it is at the
cost of diminishing the strength of the bees and the
quantity of their product. A first swarm may often
be led to throw off a cast even in the same year, but
it must be late in the season: consequently there
must be a deficiency in the store of winter provisions: before spring they dwindle and die. The
first swarm is weakened, the second is lost; but if
care had been taken to prevent their separation, there
would have been one strong stock for the following
year, which in all circumstances is infinitely better
than many weak ones.

Mr. Isaac, in his useful little tract, gives the following definition of a few APIARIAN TECHNICALITIES.
I copy them as being rather more precise than those
to which I have been generally accustomed: "By
colonies, are to be understood bees in double or treble
hives. *Stocks* designate bees generally at the end of
the season. All bees, from the season of hiving till
its conclusion at Michaelmas, are called *swarms*;
subsequently *stocks*, if in single hives; *colonies*, if in
double. A swarm having thrown out a swarm, becomes then a *stock*, although it may have been hived
but a few weeks. Such superabundant swarming

in this climate is disadvantageous. Swarming generally continues between two and three weeks."

Mr. Brown, of Renfrew, N. B., had a hive which cast *three* swarms in 1807, *five* swarms in 1808, *three* swarms in 1809, and *four* swarms in 1810, the parent hive still in good strength. In 1826, Mr. E. Day, of Coldblow farm, Hucking, took from fourteen stocks of bees 576 lbs. of honey.

Such examples as these, and even in favourable circumstances they are rare, are apt to lead the young Apiarian astray, but his great object should be to prevent the breaking-up of his stock into fragments; to keep it entire, and hold it together as much as possible, which will secure him against many unforeseen contingencies, save him much anxiety, trouble, and expense, while eventually it leads to the greatest amount of profit.

Gelieu justly observes, "In the swarming season the strong hives are almost entirely filled with brood combs. At that time also honey becomes abundant, and when fine days succeed each other, the working-bees amass an astonishing quantity. But where is it to be stored? Must they wait till the young bees have left the brood cells, by which time the early flowers will be withered? What is to be done in this dilemma? Mark the resources of the industrious bees. They search in the neighbourhood where they may deposit their honey until the young shall have left the combs in which they were hatched. If they fail in this object, they crowd together in the front of their habitation, forming prodigious clusters.

It is not uncommon to see them building combs on the outsides."

By increasing their accommodation in their present home, and lessening the temperature by ventilation, they would be saved all the hurry and hubbub, the bustle and the bother of "a flitting," two of which are said to be to ourselves worse than a fire, and one to them we are assured must be as bad as a thunder shower. Let it be avoided by all means. They are industrious creatures, but the season of swarming is to them an idle and uncomfortable period. The collecting of honey, while all nature is inviting them to the congenial task, is laid aside, and for one plain reason—because they have no room wherewithal to store it.

The months of May and June are the periods of swarming, but the precise departure of the swarm depends in a great measure on the state of the weather. The swarming season is the most important and anxious period of the labours of the Apiarian, for on its successful issue depends the chief part of his profit. It should be the aim of every keeper of bees to make himself thoroughly acquainted with the chief symptoms of the departure of a swarm, for his ignorance on this point will expose him to certain loss. Circumstances may possibly so combine as that the most experienced Apiarian may be mistaken in his calculations, but in the majority of cases the prognostics of a swarm are so decisive, that the precise period of its departure can be definitely fixed.

The symptoms indicative of swarming are various. Clustering outside of the hive is not an infallible sign, for unless a queen be ready, however much they may be annoyed for want of room, they may remain in that position for weeks. According to Reaumur, if on any particular day there is little egress from a hive, whence they were seen previously issuing in great numbers, it may be considered as indubitable that the period of swarming is at hand. The reason is obvious,—the bees, aware that they are about to depart, consider it unnecessary to labour for furnishing a habitation which they are no longer to occupy, and therefore remain at home. Another sign is a general hum in the evening, continued during night. On placing the ear close to the hive, clear and sharp sounds may be distinguished. On the following day numbers may be seen at the mouth of the hive uttering notes of alarm; and if no business seems to be going on in the interior, a young queen only requires to come forth to be followed by a numerous retinue. But the only remedy for the infallibility of these is to keep a strict watch, otherwise the swarm may be completely lost, or go to increase the stock of some distant neighbour.

When the swarming does take place, the best plan is to leave the bees as much as possible to themselves; the rattling of peas and the throwing of water being practices "more honoured in the breach, than in the observance." In this respect, in our own experience, we have been peculiarly fortunate, never having run any risk or been put to much trouble with one of our swarms. This we attribute in a great measure to our having followed the general axiom now stated; and the only instances in which we departed from it was, when by their appearing to wheel a high flight in the air, as if bent on a distant flight, we threw up some fine sand among the lower strata, where the queen, from her tardiness of flight, was most likely to be; when the whole have darted down, and clustered in the course of an instant upon the nearest shrub. If there are low trees or bushes near the hive, they will choose them, and but seldom desire a long journey. We have known, during a succession of years, each swarm from the same stock clustering invariably upon the same branch of the same tree. If it can be done conveniently, the hive for their reception—having the concave top rubbed with a little ale and sugar—should be placed immediately above them, when they will speedily begin to ascend. A white cloth should be thrown over the hive, and in the evening all will be found snugly housed, their operations already commenced, and prepared to be placed on their permanent pedestal. This in general in our experience we have been able to accomplish, but if it is necessary to place the hive under the cluster, the bees must be swept into it by a goose-wing or some other convenient instrument.

Sometimes when a swarm is hovering in the air, it divides, and a part falls to the ground. This should be carefully examined, for the queen may perchance be among them. If so, she should immediately be placed in the empty hive, and if but a few see her, they will instantly join her, followed by the whole host. If another swarm seems desirous to rise, it must be promptly stopped, as they would be apt to join, and if one of the queens is not quickly slain in battle, a war of uncompromising extermination would take place between the rival clans.

3. *Hives.*—Bees are of themselves in a state of nature at no loss in procuring a suitable residence. They collect their stores in the fissures of rocks and in the hollows of decayed trees. The climate, the locality, and the taste of the proprietor, must modify the nature of their habitation in a domesticated state. Bees have a wonderful facility, founded on the sagacity of their nature, in adapting their works to the form of their dwelling, although it has been positively affirmed by Gelieu that they form more honey in a shallow vessel than in a very deep one, but on this point we cannot decide.

In the purchase of stocks, the following essential points should be attended to, without a knowledge of which the young Apiarian will find himself deceived at the very moment when his expectations of ultimate success are raised to the highest pitch. It is with a bee-hive as with a wife, never take one on the recommendation of another person, but be your own judge of its merits and defects. If it be your intention to purchase a stock, repair to the garden in which it stands, about the middle of the day, and, placing yourself before it, pay particular attention to the action of the bees. If you observe them crowding in and out of the hive, and a considerable number of them having little yellow pellets or balls on their hinder legs, a very favourable opinion may be formed of the health and condition of the interior, and especially of the prolific state of the queen. If

3

the examination take place previously to the swarming season, pay particular attention to the number of drones : this is an infallible criterion of the populousness of the hive, and the purchaser may then confidently look forward to the possession of the usual swarms.

If, on the other hand, the examination take place in the autumn, the previous massacre of the drones must be ascertained ; the omission of this act on the part of the bees, is a certain sign of some radical defect, most probably on the part of the queen, and the prospect of the bees surviving the winter becomes thereby highly problematical. If the bees appear irascible and bold in their attacks on their enemies, particularly the wasp, it is a good sign ot their condition if on their return from the fields their bodies appear cylindrical. it is certain proof that the bees are busy in the collection of honey, and consequently a good estimate may be formed of the interior richness of the hive. In regard to the exterior of the hive, on no account select one which is old and decayed, as such hives are always infested with vermin. No prudent apiarian will ever put a swarm into an old hive, and in this respect it must be admitted that in a great degree the most culpable carelessness exists on the part of cottagers, who, perhaps, from a principle of false economy, put their swarms into old and rotten hives rather than be at the expense of purchasing new ones.

Hives either stand in a bee-house, box, or shed, or under a thatched or other kind of roof. The stand on which the hive is placed should always be kept clean, particularly so in the spring, at the commencement of the working season. If it be at times sprinkled with a little salt, it will be very conducive to the health of the bees. In short, all impurities should be removed from within and without the hive, in order to save the cleanly insects the unprofitable labour of the removal of nuisances.

The hives most generally used in England, and which are recommended by Cobbet as the best, are made of straw, of a bell-shape, but with no arrangement for ventilation or enlargement. Among cottagers, on account of their cheapness, these hives still command a preference, notwithstanding the more improved form and material introduced in modern times. Undressed rye straw serves best for their construction: they should be about thirteen inches wide at the bottom, and about nine at the top, and it would be an improvement to have them somewhat thicker than they are generally made at present. It is customary to pass sticks through them at right angles for the purpose of supporting the combs, but as these rather obstruct the bees in their operations, the end would be better gained by making the lower part narrower. This could be easily managed by making the base of the hive a stout wooden hoop, to which the lower circumference might be fitted, allowing the hive to bulge out as it approached the top. This is recommended by Dr. Bevan, who says, that this hoop should be perforated through its whole course in an oblique direction, "the perforations so distant from each other as to cause all the stitches of the hive to range in a uniform manner," and thus to be wrought into the lower band. The hoop makes the hive more durable, more steady, and more easily moved. A circular piece of wood, about three inches in diameter, with an inch hole in the centre, should be wrought into the crown. Through this opening the bees may be fed more advantageously than at the entrance, and it can be so far serviceable for ventilating the hive. When not required for either of these purposes, it can easily be plugged up, or covered with a bit of tin. Straw hives are often covered with an earthen pan; in Scotland a mere sod or thatch of straw is often used, which can neither be said to be tidy nor tasteful, and, eke, dirty and dangerous. At all events, the covering, whatever it is, should always shape outwards, to carry off all moisture, against which too much precaution cannot be used; and of whatever materials the hives may be composed, they should be well painted at first, and at regular intervals afterwards, "for," as Mr. Payne says, "hives managed on the depriving system are expected to last from 15 to 20 years."

Wooden hives or boxes are now almost invariably employed by the best bee cultivators, for, however those of straw may form a ready resource to the cottager, wooden ones are not only cheaper in the end from their greater durability, but more profitable at first from their square form, affording greater facilities for the more economical arrangement of the combs. The boxes may be made of any wood if it is dry, well seasoned, well joined, and not resinous. The size must depend on the number of bees it is to contain, and that depends much upon the honey-pasturage of the district. Ten or twelve inches square, and an inch thick, are the fair dimensions. The top should project about an inch, both for ornament and utility,—also a hole at the top for feeding, and of size sufficient to insert a bell-glass, with one at the top for ventilation. There may be a window, both in front and behind, for the purpose of inspection, which ought to be furnished with zinc shutters, to slide closely up and down in a groove. Hives of this kind require to be placed under a cover or shed, to protect them from the rain and the heat of the sun.

When a number of hives are kept, they may be placed on shelves in a row, one over the other, and thus one roof may be made to cover nine as easily as three, and twelve as easily as four. This may be distinctly understood by the annexed figure.

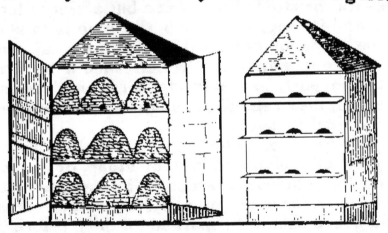

The front is a fixture, perforated by nine holes opposite to the entrance of each of the hives, with an alighting board. The back is enclosed with folding doors, on opening which the hives can either be inspected or removed. The whole should be carefully painted, and rendered wind and water tight. Should the apiary be extensive, and the hives stand in double rows, Mr. Huish advises the chequered form:

O O O O O O
O O O O O

In which mode the flight of the bees in the hinder row will not be obstructed by the front hives. A bee taking flight from the hive generally forms a considerable angle with the horizon in his ascent; and should the hive stand at too great a degree of elevation, the advantage would enable the swarm to take so extensive a flight, that they might be totally lost. But if the site be not sufficiently extensive to admit of the hives being placed in a right line, it is preferable to set them one over another in double rows. The pedestal or stool should have but a single leg or support, and its top, on which the hive is to stand, should be made of seasoned and substantial wood, which will not warp, and which should be firmly nailed to the post, in a slanting direction, in order that the rain may run off, all stagnant moisture being highly inimical to bees.

The *floor-board* on which the hives stand should literally be of wood, and not of stone, or any cold material, for obvious reasons. There must be a separate board for every hive. The weight of each hive and board should be marked on them before use. The entrance is generally cut out of the bottom of the hive, but it should rather be scooped from the surface of the board, gradually sloping upward into the hive. It ought to be made wide, as it can be contracted at any time. But a better method still is a double board, with a space in front between, and through the upper part of which a hole for entrance is cut altogether within the hive.

The hive should never be cemented to the board with mortar or clay. The bees themselves furnish the best cement: all others only serve to hasten the decay of the hive, and to breed vermin.

Hives may be enlarged in a variety of ways; by storifying, by collateral hives; by made hives, and these in multifarious modes, which we would rather trust to the practical ingenuity of our readers than minutely describe; but those who wish details, will find them amply in Huish, Nutt, Bagster, Taylor, and Jardine.

4. *Ventilators and Thermometer.* The ventilators used, and so well described by Taylor in *The Bee-Keeper's Manual,* consist of double tin or zinc tubes, both resting in the holes prepared for them on a flask or rim. "The centre tube is of one inch diameter and six inches long, with six half-inch holes dispersed over it. It is soon fixed down by the bees, and so must remain. The inner tube is of perforated zinc, with a tin projecting top as a handle, and a cap to put on or off this as required. The bees will stop up the inner tube when they can get at it, when it may be turned round a little to present a new surface. When wholly stopped, it may be withdrawn

from its place, and a new tube substituted. This may be done without the least danger to the operator; but it should be inserted carefully, to avoid crushing any bees that may have crept within the outer tube. An exit for these is afforded by a hole at the bottom. The tube that has thus been removed may be cleansed by the aid of hot water.

"In order occasionally to know the temperature of any of the boxes, a thermometer made to fit the ventilator may occasionally be inserted in it. This will at all times give facility for making accurate observations, but it is more particularly useful as a matter of precaution toward the swarming season."

An experienced apiarian, and in certain seasons, may perhaps be able to dispense with the use of the ventilator and thermometer, and by some they are denounced as an unwieldly and unnecessary apparatus, serving no important purpose in the economy of the hive. On the inexperienced, however, it cannot be too strongly impressed how important a stepping-stone they form in his progress to ultimate success—how much success and security by means of them he is able to attain—how many mistakes to avoid, and knowledge to acquire—while even without them the most skilful will never be able to proceed with the same degree of certainty, especially in that important step, the prevention of swarming; nor will bees ever work so well in a heated atmosphere as with a moderate and equable temperature. A cool store-room also contributes most essentially to the purity of the honey and the whiteness of the comb. The expense of the ventilators being so trifling, ought to form no barrier in the way of their introduction into every hive. It has been erroneously supposed and illogically argued that bees have an antipathy to ventilation, because they so carefully close up every hole through which air can be admitted, especially in the hottest weather, when a fresh supply would be most acceptable; but the truth is, they are equally careful in shutting up every crevice, whether there is any circulation through it or not. This argument, therefore, falls to the ground, and we say to every bee-holder, employ the ventilator and thermometer with all convenient speed.

5. *Feeding Apparatus.*—Too little attention is in general paid to the feeding of bees, on which account many a fine hive has been impoverished by its neglect, or destroyed by its injudicious application. According to the common process it is always a troublesome and frequently a dangerous operation; but by a certain apparatus it can be rendered equally simple and safe. The bees by means of it are fed at the top instead of the bottom of the hive. In this way, then, they may be fed in any quantity and at any time, with more convenience to themselves and no risk to the feeder. According to the description of Mr. Taylor, "it consists of a tin or zinc pan, twelve inches by seven inches on the outside, and one inch and a quarter deep, made very flat at the bottom. A partition runs the length of one side of the pan, leaving the space of an inch wide, into which the food is poured, a passage for this being left all along under the partition an eighth of an inch high. It thus finds its way into the centre,

where there is a thin perforated wooden bottom, a little raised underneath, and which floats on the food. The bees enter the pan through two holes corresponding in position with those on the top of the hive, and round the holes are rims half an inch high. A square of glass forms a cover, by means of which the bees may be seen without danger."

A wooden cover should be made to fit over the pans to prevent the access of robbers, and it ought to be high enough to receive the bell-glass, or glasses; for these are at all times best covered. An additional advantage of pans on this construction will be seen in winter, for the vapour caused by the moisture is condensed in the bells and carried away. As the exhalation rises from the bees below, it is condensed on the glass, and received in considerable quantities into the pan. In the absence of a bell-glass, the glass cover or lid to the pan may be kept in its place as a substitute, and on it a large quantity of vapour will be condensed.

6. *Miscellaneous Management.*—A great deal depends upon the position of the hive. It should have a south or south-eastern aspect, sheltered from the wind, and not in the neighbourhood of ponds or rivers, which form a watery grave to many a burdened busy bee.

In the vicinity of the hive there should be planted in large quantities crocus, single blue hepaticus, *helleborus niger*, and *tussalago petasites*, all of which flower early, and are rich in honey and farina. But the most cultivated districts are not to be compared with wild heaths, woods, and commons, or any place where white clover, saintfain, buckwheat, mustard, coleseed, &c. prevail.

A swarm should be selected early, if possible in May, for stocking a hive, which should be immediately placed in the position where it is intended to remain. The greater the mass of bees kept in one hive the better—five swarms combined not consuming more food than two. This to some appears strange, but it is not the less true, and can be easily accounted for. For the best method of uniting swarms, especially in collateral hives, see Taylor's *Bee-Keeper's Manual.* "War to the knife," should be declared against all wasps, moths, earwigs, ants, spiders, and cobwebs. Weak hives are often attacked and destroyed by strange bees, against which the best and perhaps the only security is numbers. "Union is strength." In proportion to the wealth of the colony, is the desire and the power of the bees to defend it.

"In doubling the population," says Gelieu, "I naturally conceived that we must also double the quantity of food, for I had always seen that two or three families living together used more meat than each would have done singly, however rigid their economy. The more mouths the more meat, thought I, and in consequence I augmented greatly the amount of provisions the first time I doubled a hive, but to my great astonishment, when I weighed it again in the spring, I found that the united swarms had not consumed more than each would have done singly. I could not believe my eyes, but thought there must be some mistake; nor could I be convinced until I had repeated the experiment a hundred times over, and had always the same result. After this discovery I varied my experiments, not only to convince myself of the fact, but if possible to arrive at still more extended results. I joined three hives in the autumn, by introducing into the middle one the bees of two neighbouring hives, and I found on weighing it in the spring that its inhabitants had scarcely weighed one pound more than those of hives that had not been united. I went further: having a large, well-stocked, and amply-provided hive, I added to it in the autumn, without displacing it, the swarms of four neighbouring hives, two on the right hand and two on the left, which were so scarce of provisions, that the quantity of honey that would have been necessary to keep them alive, would have far exceeded their value, and that all four would to a certainty have perished. This enormous population produced a heat so great, that during the whole of a very severe winter the bees kept up a buzzing noise, equal to that of a strong and active hive in the evening of a fine day in spring. The hive was left out all the winter, and would infallibly have perished had I shut it up. What was my astonishment on weighing it in the spring to find, that, notwithstanding it contained five families, the total diminution did not exceed what took place in my ordinary hives! It gave out excellent swarms long before any of the others, and recompensed me well for my pains."

This seeming anomaly is simply explained from the circumstance, that in a thinly-populated hive almost the whole of the bees are required at this time to feed and warm their young, and consequently little or nothing is added to the continually decreasing stock of honey and farina. When the stock is large, a great proportion can be spared to go abroad in search of food for the rising generation.

Bees individually are short-lived, but as a community they may be said to be immortal. Lord Brougham, in his " Dissertations on subjects of Science connected with Natural Theology," and whose minute details on scientific subjects make one wonder that he should be at the same time a classical scholar, an expert rhetorician, and an ingenious, if not a profound lawyer, says, " The attention which has been paid at various times to the structure and habits of the bee, is one of the most remarkable circumstances in the history of science. The ancients studied it with unusual minuteness, although being, generally speaking, indifferent observers of facts, they made but little progress in discovering the economy of this insect. Of the observations of Aristomachus, who spent sixty years, it is said, in the study of the subject, we know nothing; nor of those that were made by Philissus, who passed his life in the woods for the purpose of examining this insect's habits; but Pliny informs us that both of them wrote works upon it. Aristotle's three chapters on bees and wasps contain little more than the ordinary observations, mixed up with an unusual portion of vulgar and even gross errors. How much he attended to the subject is, however, manifest from the extent of the first of these chapters, which is of great length. Some mathematical writers studied the form of the cells, and established one or two of the fundamental propositions respecting the economy of labour and wax, resulting from the plan of the structure. The application of modern naturalists to the inquiry, is to be dated from the beginning of the eighteenth century, when Maraldi examined it with his accustomed care, and Reaumur afterwards, as we have seen, carried his investigations much farther. The interest of the subject seemed to increase with the progress made in these inquiries, and about the year 1765 a Society was formed at Little Baut-zen, in Upper Lusatia, whose sole object was the study of bees. It was formed under the patronage of the Elector of Saxony. The celebrated Schirach was one of its original members, and soon after its establishment he made his famous discovery of the power which the bees have to supply the loss of their Queen, by forming a large cell out of three common ones, and feeding the grub of a worker upon royal jelly; a discovery so startling to naturalists, that Bonnet, in 1769, earnestly urged the Society not to lower its credit by countenancing such a wild error, which he regarded as repugnant to all we know of the habits of insects,—admitting, however, that he should not be so incredulous of any observations tending to prove the propagation of the race of the Queen bee without any co-operation of a male, a no-tion since shown by Huber to be wholly chimerical. In 1771, a second institution under the Elector Pala-tine's patronage, with the same limited object, but founded at Lauter, and of which Rien, scarcely less known in this branch of science than Schirach, was a member.

"The greatest progress, however, was afterwards made by Huber, whose discoveries, especially of the Queen Bee's mode of impregnation, the slaughter of the drones or males, and the mode of working, have justly gained him a very high place among natural-ists. Nor are his discoveries of the secretion of wax from saccharine matter, the nature of propolis and the nature of wax for building, to be reckoned less important. For these truths the way had been led by John Hunter, whose vigorous and original genius never was directed to the cultivation of any subject without reaping a harvest of discovery. Since the time of Hunter and Huber no progress has been made in this branch of knowledge." The-oretically, Lord Brougham and Vaux is in all this, and especially in his last statement, correct; but after the perusal of our petty, but pretty work, it is hoped that he will be found altogether practically wrong, by the spread and improvement of bee-culture here and there and every where.

THE PIGEON.

———

1. *Nature of the Pigeon.*—The pigeon can be easily naturalized in every climate, with the exception of the frigid zones. Towards the two poles it is seldom to be found, and never thrives or propagates, while it is prosperous in temperate regions—the burning sun of the tropics rather improving than impairing its natural constitution ; but the wild pigeons of cold countries always emigrate towards the south on the approach of winter.

In a civilized and improved condition, they appear, of all the feathered tribes, more subject to the process of amelioration, than when in a state of nature. The superiority of the one to the other, is evidenced by the fact, that in the natural state they are difficult to be caught, and few in numbers, but when domesticated, and brought up under the fostering hand of man, they increase in endless varieties of plumage and of form.

As emblematical of beauty, and innocence, they have always ranked among the feathered favourites of mankind ; in eastern countries, they are regarded not only as objects of religious superstition, but held

4

in veneration, as the harbingers, or the emblems, of peace and love.

II. *Political view of the Pigeon.*—A question has been raised regarding the national profit, or loss, which might arise from encouraging an extensive breed of Pigeons. On this point, both agriculturists, men of science, and amateurs, have differed in opinion, but it will be found, that no respectable antagonist to their partial propagation has appeared. We must confess, however, that Mr. Du-harnel, the apologist for the Dove tribes, has not been a very successful advocate. He avers, that pigeons do not feed upon green corn—that their bills have not sufficient power to dig for seeds in the earth, and that they only pick up scattered grains, which would else be wasted, or become the prey of other birds. From the season of the corn appearing, he says, pigeons subsist principally upon the seeds of weeds, the multiplication and spread of which they must, in consequence, greatly prevent.

Another writer has of late introduced a story of the farmers in a certain district in England, who, finding their corn and pulse crops greatly reduced, attributed it to the vast quantity of pigeons kept among them, which, on this account, by a general resolution, they agreed to destroy. A few seasons afterwards, it seems they found their lands so exhausted, and their crops so overrun with weeds, that they came to a general wish for their pigeons back again. "Now," says Mowbray, "this is either a lame story, or the farmers implicated were very lame farmers, if they did not know how to weed their land, without the assistance of agents the use of which must cost them so considerable a part of their crops." Last year, a farmer in Kent shot a wood-pigeon, from the crop of which he extracted nine hundred and twenty-six clavels of wheat, which he sowed, and obtained from them a harvest of one gallon three quarts of wheat. Every man, in the least acquainted with country affairs, is aware of the immense damage done to the crops of corn, beans, peas, and tares, by pigeons. A sufficient proof of this may be found in the reduction of the number of dove-cots throughout all countries where agriculture is best known, valued, and practised. Every one will judge for himself of the degree of credit due to the following statement, extracted from Mr. Vancouver's valuable survey of the county of Devon :

"Pigeons often fly to a great distance for their food, and when they can find corn to eat, seldom prey upon anything else. They begin to eat corn about the middle of July, and rarely want the same food, all the stacks in the straw-yards, or in the fields, until the end of barley sowing, which is about old May-day, and which includes a period of two hundred and eighty days, or better than three quarters of the year, being during that period laid under contribution; living the rest of the time upon the seeds of weeds and bentings. It is somewhere stated, that in England and in Wales there are twenty thousand dove-houses, averaging each at about one hundred pair of old pigeons. Taking this estimation at three-fourths, it will equal one million one hundred and twenty-five pair of dove-house pigeons, in England and Wales. These will consume, with what they carry home to their young, one pint of corn per pair daily, and for one hundred and forty days, being half the period during which they are supposed to subsist upon corn, amounts to one hundred and fifty-seven millions five hundred thousand pints of corn, consumed annually throughout England and Wales by pigeons." In Scotland, the mania for rearing immense flocks of pigeons is now nearly extinct. They seem to have been kept in the capacity, and to have performed the duty of the gleaners, of former days. No costly cote built for their accommodation, is now almost any where to be seen, except some lonely moss-o'ergrown fabric, venerable for its age, and perhaps valuable to the antiquary, but affording accommodation to no living creature except the owl, the sparrow, and the bat, and destined ere long to crumble into irremediable ruins. This is as it should be ; for although pigeons are always beautiful they are only valuable in their proper place. They can easily be kept in sufficient numbers, and propagated to a sufficient extent, without all this cumbrous machinery ; but many of our ancestors, and even some antiquated proprietors of the present day, seemed to have imagined that the *staff of life* was *pigeon-pie*, and that it should form the daily food of mankind. But all this is fast, and for ever, passing away. In towns they can do no harm, except to the purse of the proprietor, who must furnish the principal part of their food. And they must be considered valuable, either in town or country, as they can pick up from the street or the road many a precious pile of grain, which would be otherwise irretrievably lost. Keeping immense flocks, is the only evil.

On a general view of the subject, it appears that the dove-house system has ever been, in many cases, one of extreme injustice, as well as impolicy, in point of national advantage; since great flocks may be maintained at the expense of persons having no property in them, and to whom they afford no profit. But as neither the public nor individuals will consent to be deprived of the enjoyment of this ancient luxury, the fairest mode appears to be the regular feeding of pigeons, by their proprietors, which in almost every instance so attaches them to home, that there is often, not only a necessity of driving them out for exercise, but the prevention of loss from their not straying. This plan should, of course, be more punctually observed in seed time, and towards the approach of the corn crops to maturity, but after reaping, it may of course in some measure be dispensed with.

8. *Varieties of the Pigeon.*—Buffon, in his enumeration, mentions upwards of thirty varieties; which, according to his usual systematical method, is probably more remarkable for convenience than for accuracy, but which he traces to one common origin: the *Stock Dove*, or common wild pigeon, (*Columba anas.*)

The varieties of colour and form which we witness he attributes to human contrivance and fancy. There exist, nevertheless, essential specific differences in these birds, which seem rather attributable to the nature of the region, soil, or climate, to which they are indigenous, than to the art of man.

Respecting the origin of the different species of the pigeon, (and of no one kind are there so many varieties known to us,) another opinion prevails; some naturalists deriving it from the rock pigeon, (*Columba Linia.*) I certainly incline towards the latter opinion, as the habits of the Rock Dove are closely allied to those of the dove-house pigeon, and a cross between the Dragoon and Rock Dove may be effected, while I believe the young of the Stock Dove has never yet been subjected to the confinement of the loft.

The Stock Dove, or original of the pigeon genus, according to Buffon, in its natural or wild state, is thus described; " with a fine neck of a reddish gold colour, its wings marked with two black bars, one on the quill feathers, and the other on the covert; the back white, and the tail barred near the end with black." The *Ring Dove* is yet held by naturalists to be distinct from the *Stock Dove,* and it would seem that the *Turtle Dove* is equally so from both. In this country the *Blue Dove* (house pigeon) is the most common, and the only species of these are the *Ring Doves*, or wood pigeons, and the *Turtle Doves*,) which are to be found in all parts of Southern Britain, breeding during the spring and summer, and retiring to the deepest recesses of the woods in the winter season, whence, probably, the Turtle has been supposed to emigrate. I am assured by a Spanish gentleman, that in Barbary they have pigeons equal in size to fowls, but incapable of flight.

Throughout the woods and plantations on the domain of Warwick Castle, the Turtle Dove abounds in multitudes, flying in pairs, and lighting on the turrets of the castle. Their loud and mournful cooing is heard on the road at a considerable distance. Much pains have been taken, hitherto ineffectually, to reduce their numbers.

The autumnal markets in the metropolis, and in most large towns, generally exhibit a large supply of *Wood Pigeons.* They assemble in large flocks, and take refuge during night in thick coverts, perching on the middle branches and top of the oak tree. As to the sport of shooting wood pigeons, the wintry and boisterous evenings in November are the most appropriate, when they are to be found roosting with their faces to windward, and the sportsman, generally approaching behind them, hidden by the lower foliage, and aided also from its rustling, obtains a fair chance of success, though the Ring Dove is particularly shy and watchful. This is a sport by which any one, taking his stand in the twilight, may shoot the birds sitting or flying, and, without much exertion, soon have his bags well filled.

The flesh of the wood-pigeon is in perfection about the end of Summer and during Autumn, from their ability in those seasons to procure the most fattening food. While in winter, feeding on cole-warts or any green food they can find, makes their flesh loose and bitter, but their large size would be

increased by domestication, and the experiment must
be successful.   At Pamber House, Herts, according
to Mowbray, there had been, immemorially, an annual
nest of wood-pigeons in a large yew-tree, said to be
three centuries old, which grew in the garden within a few yards of the house.   We seldom saw the
old birds, as they used the utmost vigilance.   They
are well supplied with them from the neighbouring
forest.   In 1827, immense flocks of wood-pigeons,
to the computed number of two thousand in one field,
were seen upon the lands near Chichester.   Sir H.
Fisher's keeper killed sixty couple in one day.

Both in the ancient and modern world this beautiful and variegated genus of birds has been cherished
by man as a source of amusement and gratification
to the eye, as well as profit, in the article of provision for the table.   Besides, it was reckoned by certain nations of antiquity unlawful to deprive them
of life.   The useful qualification of Messenger, ap-
pertaining to the Asiatic and African species of the
pigeon, is of great antiquity : and we read, in the
time of the Crusades, of an Arabian prince who had
a sort of telegraphic communication kept up in his
dominions through the medium of pigeons, that
carried letters, and were regularly relieved at appointed posts.   From these, doubtless, the breed
celebrated in Europe under the name of the Carrier
has proceeded.   In modern times, those varieties
which are kept for the purpose of amusement and
show, are styled *Fancy Breeds*, and they form a distinct article of commerce in cities and great towns,
the varieties, as they chance to be in fashion, bring-

ing a considerable price. From the earliest times the pigeon fanciers of London have had a club, in which premiums are awarded, and the notable science of the fancy, through the method of crossing colours and forms, is promoted and perpetuated. The chief objects of the fancy have hitherto been those varieties styled *Almond* (probably ermine,) *Tumblers, Carriers,* and the birds with great crops, the most fashionable variety of which is the *Pouting Horseman.* The specific merits of these breeds are indicated by their names. The tumbler exercises his faculty in the air, but is chiefly valued for his peculiar form and variegated plumage. The Carrier, as a messenger, cuts the air with almost inconceivable swiftness. This is the *columba tabellaria,* the famous carrier, or messenger, between Aleppo and Alexandria in Egypt. The Pouter extends his crop to a size attractive to curiosity, and by his grotesque attitudes and familiarity with man, engages his attention. Half a century since, the pigeon *Fancy* was in higher estimation than at present, then : the almond tumbler was in its greatest vogue ; sums to the amount of twenty or thirty guineas each being the general price of superior cocks of that breed, such as in the present time would not bring more than five. The pigeon shops invariably appear the abode of poverty and wretchedness, and the poor unfortunate birds, crammed into baskets and narrow coops, obviously partake of the calamity in the fullest measure. This fancy is much indulged in with certain of the lower classes, in the metropolis, and it is to be regretted that so much of their time is spent in the practice of entrapping stray pigeons and leading the fanciers from honest industry to loose and irregular habits.

It would be useless to assign a reason why one particular breed out of so many species should alone possess the peculiar knowledge and instinct of the carrier. We must content ourselves without diving too far into the hidden mysteries of nature, and ascribe that wonderful facility to the same Power that guides the swallow and other birds of passage across the waters of the Atlantic to our shores, or conducts them, each succeeding spring, to the same spot where for previous seasons they have reared their young.

Tumblers by their flight are a source of great enjoyment to the fanciers, for in addition to their tumbling they will rise to so great a height in the air as to appear like a speck, or become altogether imperceptible. If of a good kind, and well familiarized to one another, they will in their flight keep in so close company that a dozen of them may be covered with a handkerchief. If the weather be fine and clear, they will keep upon the wing for four or five hours at a time, the favourite set seldom or never tumbling except when about to rise, or when coming down to pitch.

Tumblers show in their plumage an endless variegation of shade—reds, yellows, blues, duns, blacks, whites, and silvers. No expense should be spared at first for the purchase of two or more birds accustomed to very high flying, as they will be of infinite use afterwards, in teaching the young ones to be lofty soarers. After the pigeons have been accustomed to their habitations, they should be turned out only once a day in a clear grey morning, when there is neither mist nor wind, taking care to spread out for them on their return a plentiful repast of rape or canary seed, to entice then home, and afterwards shutting them up for the rest of the day. They should, for an obvious reason, be closely confined when with egg.

The Carrier was called by some of the old fanciers, the King of Pigeons. It is remarkable for the fleshy protuberance called the wattle on the lower part of the head. These triple properties have been enumerated as indicative of its excellence—three in the head, three in the eye, three in the wattle, and three in the beak. The head should be flat, straight, and long ; the eye broad, circular, and uniform ; the wattle broad across the beak, short from the head to the bill, and leaning forward ; the beak long, straight, and thick. Pigeon jockeyship sometimes has attempted to imitate these qualities artificially, and to palm upon the inexperienced inferior birds at the price of the best. The length and thinness of the neck are marks of its elegance.

The *Horseman* is supposed to be a bastard between the Tumbler and Carrier : they are chiefly used at present for deciding bets, and carrying letters, the pure Carrier being so exceedingly scarce.

Dragoons were originally bred between the Horseman and Carrier ; they are very strong and useful birds ; being prolific breeders, and good nurses, they are frequently kept as feeders to rear young Pouters,

Leghorn runts, &c. For a distance of fifteen or twenty miles, the Dragoon is said to be more rapid than the Horseman, but cannot keep up its superiority in a longer flight.

But while on this part of our subject, it would not be doing justice to our readers, whether old or young, and it would be denying to ourselves a gratification, not to quote here the remarks of a correspondent, who signs himself *Toho,* in the New Sporting Magazine for June, 1839. They are at once practical and scientific, and cannot fail to be interesting to every possessor of a pigeon loft, who wishes to improve the breed or the value of his stocks. He says with regard to this beautiful and valuable variety :

" The first property of a Carrier is the length of their flight or wing feathers, and the distance or length from the base of the bill to the end, which should always taper gradually. The colour is the next, and though fanciers disagree on this point, I prefer a blue to any other, as I have generally found them hardier and swifter than the blacks or duns, but, like dogs, good pigeons are to be found of all colours. Firmness of feather always indicates a good constitution. The age may be guessed by the size of the wattle, and the heavy appearance of the bird.

" The Antwerps are a later introduction into this country, and their name bespeaks their origin. I believe little was known of them before the famous Antwerp match in July, 1830, when 110 birds were tossed from the yard of a noted fancier in the Borough. The first bird reached Antwerp, a distance

of 186 miles, in five hours and a half, and gained the
gold medal; out of the 110, about 100 reached home.
To the eye of any one who has been solely accustomed to the English Carrier, they possess but little
recommendation, but the fancier soon detects the
points of speed and beauty, in the fine and lengthy
shape of the bird. They are of many colours,
but I have found none better than the nearly reds
and blues. This bird, in my opinion, is equal to the
Horseman in sagacity and speed, and altogether, I
prefer them to any other kind.

"The pigeon loft should always, if possible, face
the west or south, be high and roomy, with railed pens
to shut in birds for matching in the spring, or other
purposes, kept well lime-washed, which will both
destroy the insects, and keep it cool, and it should
be repeatedly cleaned out. A glass tile or two in the
roof, if it is a slanting one, will be useful to light
the loft.

There must be a railed trap projecting in front,
so that the birds may go out from the loft, and the front
of the trap will let down and pull up, by means of
a spring inside. This is the dormer, and in most
large lofts is out of the top of the roof. When the
trap is shut the birds will come in at the wires,
which open inwards to the loft, on a pivot, which is
called the bolting wire.

Of course, in stocking a loft, all depends upon
its size and the taste of the fancier. I should say,
six couples of Dragoons and strong Horsemen, and
two couples of Beards well matched, and purchased
in the spring, will be a good breeding supply. These

must be shut in the loft for breeding, and the young birds flown. They will begin breeding about the end of February, and continue till October ; I would however, for flying, save no kinds till May. The old bird sits eighteen days, and the male relieves the female. Peas form their chief food, but tares will be found best for the young ones till they leave the nest. While watching the birds, give a little hemp-seed. Often before the young birds leave the nest, the old ones will lay again. As soon as the young can fly, they should be allowed to bask in the dormer, and when they have gained confidence, they will join the flight. After they have become well accustomed to the loft, and are able to keep pretty well with the flight, take them about half a mile from the loft in a bag made of coarse canvass, to hold two birds, with a little straw, and toss them ; repeat the same distance for a few days, and gradually increase it up to five miles. After this they are pretty perfect, and two or three miles may be added to the distance every day. If your loft be near a high road, a great advantage will be found by giving the birds to the coachmen to toss. There are many ways of marking birds. I generally make a little notch in the beak or between the toes, in the same manner as game fowls. A little stamp with the initials of the name, to mark them in red on the tail and pinion feathers, will be useful till the birds moult. In tossing a bird, always clear its wings and feet, and holding it round the body and legs with one hand, throw it well up,—never near any trees, as the young ones will frequently perch and there remain.

The speed of the Carrier has perhaps never been ascertained. I have had them come seven miles, by the *road*, in five minutes, and forty miles in the hour is generally done; but too much depends upon circumstances to give any opinion.

If a bird is going to do a large distance, it should never be over-fed the night previous, but shut up in a dark pen. If possible, choose a clear day for tossing, for nothing beats pigeons like wind and fog. A real Carrier will seldom stop till he reaches home. If they are regularly flown, well fed and watered, and kept clean, few diseases will be known in the loft. Let them have a large tin pan to wash in, change the water every day, and a lump of salt to peck at.

The canker in the wattle is their worst disease, and frequently arises from dirt or from the birds fighting. The best cure is a piece of bitter aloes of the size of a pea, given inwardly, and the day after wash the wattle with warm water, and in the evening wash the sore with lead ammoniac, and burnt alum, mixed with lemon juice, till cured. Tobacco smoke will be found useful to clear the loft from vermin.

The value of birds will frequently depend more on the fancy of the buyer, than on their real merit. In first stocking a loft, I would never be too particular about price, as a good breeding stock is worth more than half the latter. It would be difficult to fix any price as a general guide; I have known Horsemen fetch £5 a pair, though good ones may be bought for £2, and Dragoons will fetch all prices from 5s to £5 a couple. Beards are usually the cheapest, and Antwerps are to be bought at few fanciers, and frequently bring high prices. Of course much depends upon the shape and colour, but birds of a good strain will always fetch their price among the fancy.

I shall confine my remarks to the flyers, and say nothing about the *tory* kinds, which include Tumblers, Pouters, Jacobins, and many other species, which are held by their respective fanciers in as high estimation as the best Carriers. Of the whole species, Pouters fetch the highest prices. An amateur, who has never attended a London pigeon show, would be astonished at the prices set on the birds by their owners; and I know no prettier sight than a pen of good Horsemen or Dragoons.

Like all other fancies, that of the pigeon will be found both troublesome and expensive; but this will be fully compensated for, by the amusement afforded in rearing and flying the birds, and I think that every real lover of this bird will agree with me, that an hour may be spent much less profitably and usefully, than in the pigeon loft.

The Pouter is a very common but most interesting bird. It is remarkable for its local attachment, and although not a good breeder, and exceedingly apt to degenerate, it is very useful about the pigeon-house, by leading the other birds to form a stronger house and home. Some of them can distend their crops to a very great size, so much so as frequently to overbalance themselves. By judicious crossing and patient perseverance, some fanciers have brought these birds to so high a point of perfection as to sell them for twenty guineas a pair. They are very bad nurses, and it is difficult to rear their young without the aid of the Dragoon. When a Pouter has laid an egg at the same time with a Dragoon, they should be carefully transferred from the one to the other, it being necessary to allow the Pouter to sit, otherwise she would continue to lay, which in a short time would cause her emaciation and death. If bred in and in, they quickly degenerate and become worthless, new kinds must therefore be got by purchase or exchange, to prevent the deteriorating effects of too close a consanguineous connexion. The contrary is the case with the Almond Tumbler, which, the more it is bred in and in, only diminishes in size, and is accordingly enhanced in beauty and value.

The *Fan-tail* is a very beautiful bird, sometimes, on account of its frequent tremulous movement of the neck, called the Broadtailed Shaker. When perfect, its tail consists of not less than twenty-four or more than thirty-six feathers, which it keeps spread and always erect, for if they are but for once allowed to drop, it is a fault never overlooked and never forgiven. A very slender-necked, full-breasted, and large-tailed bird, carrying the latter gracefully, is of very great value. The plumage is agreeably white, but there is also a great variety of colours.

The *Jacobine* is a bird very scarce, and difficult to be found of a good sort. It is sometimes called Jack, and is a very small bird. It has a range of inverted feathers on the back of the head, somewhat resembling in form the cowl of a monk, or the ruff of

5

a cavalier, and hence its name. This range of feathers is called the hood—and the closer and more compact it grows to the head the greater is the value of the bird. The lower part of what is called the chain and the feathers that compass it, should be short and thick. There is a great variety of colour among them, but the yellows always obtain precedence.

Besides these we have enumerated, an almost endless variety of names has been given to some where the shades of difference are very slight. With these the young pigeon-keeper should have as little to do as possible. Even with the commonest assortment he can buy at the market or from a companion, he will soon have a sufficient variety, and many to please his eye with sufficient beauty ; and if it is necessary to assign them names, he can easily baptize them himself without consulting the vocabularies of the London fanciers.

Plucking *one* of the wings of old strangers to induce them to haunt or to prevent them from their vagabondizing propensities, sometimes manifested by old inmates, is better than cutting, as their power of flight comes on gradually as the feathers grow, and they become familiar with and fond of the features of the locality within a limited range of which they have thus been for a time confined. We have almost always seen this mode succeed in our own experience, although the reports of others all tend to the superiority of endeavouring to haunt young in preference to old birds, which is certainly surer and safer, but the other may also be tried, as the old ones may begin to breed as soon as their wing is grown, which only takes about a month, whereas six times that period must be waited for before eggs can be expected from the young ones. If a hen happens to be lost, it is seldom that the cock remains long behind,—but the very contrary happens with the loss of the cock. The hen sets out in search of a mate, and she will soon be seen wiling a male companion—widowed in all probability in some other dovecote—homeward to her own residence, where they speedily pair.

4. *Diseases of Pigeons.*—The most of fancy pigeons being monstrous productions, are peculiarly subject to disease. Girton enumerates upwards of a dozen, with their appropriate remedies, including corruption of the egg in uterus from over-high feeding,—a gorged crop, from voracious feeding,—insects, from filthiness in the pigeon-houses,—and the canker, from cocks fighting with each other. Little can be done in the way of curing these diseases, except by their recurrence to proper regimen, and if this does not produce the desired effect, it is better to put the bird *hors de peine,* both for the sake of humanity and to prevent the spread of infection. Fortunately the common pigeon, reared for the sake of the table, is but little liable to any of these disorders.

5. *Laws regarding Pigeons.*—By the 1 of James, chap. 27, shooting, or destroying pigeons by other means, is, on the evidence of two witnesses, punishable by a fine of 20 shillings for every bird killed or taken; and by the 2 of George III. c. 29, the same of-

fence may be proved by one witness, and the fine is 20 shillings to the prosecutor.

According to 7 and 8 Geo. 4, c. 29, sect. 33, persons unlawfully killing, wounding, or taking any house-dove or pigeon, under such circumstances as do not amount to larceny, at common law, shall forfeit over and above the value of the bird, any sum not exceeding forty shillings. Occupiers of land may lawfully kill pigeons destroying corn.

At the Westminster Court of Requests, in February, 1829, a decision was made against TRAPPING pigeons, the defendant being amerced in the price of the birds he had entrapped.

Any lord of the manor, or freeholder, may build a pigeon-house on his own land, but it cannot be done by the tenant without the lord's permission. Shooting or killing within a certain distance of the pigeon-house, renders the transgressor liable to forfeiture.

The remarks of Mr. Cobbet, on the subject of pigeons, are very sensible, short, founded on good authority, and worthy of attention.

"A few of them may be kept," he says, "about any cottage, for they are kept even in towns by labourers and artizans. They cause but little trouble. They take care of their own young, and they do not scratch, or do any other mischief in gardens. They want feeding with tares, peas, or small beans ; and buck-wheat is very good for them. To *begin* keeping them, they must not have *flown at large* before you get them. You must keep them for two or three days shut into the place which is to be their home ; and then they may be let out, and will never leave

you, as long as they can get proper food, and are un-
disturbed by vermin, or unannoyed exceedingly by
lice. The common dove-house pigeons are the best
to keep. They breed oftenest, and feed their young
ones best. They begin to breed at about *nine months
old*, and if well kept, they will give you eight or
nine pair in the year. Any little place, a shelf in
the cow shed ; a board or two under the eaves of the
house ; or, in-short, any place under cover, even on
the ground floor, they will sit and hatch and breed up
their young ones in.

" It is not supposed that there could be much *profit*
attached to them ; but they are of this use. they
are very pretty creatures ; very interesting in their
manners ;. they are an object to delight *children*, and
to give them the *early habit* of fondness for animals
and of *setting a value* on them, which, as I have often
had to observe before, is a very great thing. A considerable part of all the *property* of a nation consists
of animals. Of course a proportionate part of the
cares and labours of a people appertains to the breeding and bringing to perfection those animals ; and, if
you consult your experience, you will find that a la-
bourer is, generally speaking, of value in proportion
as he is worthy of being intrusted with the care of
animals. The most careless fellow cannot *hurt* a
hedge or ditch ; but to trust him with the *team* or the
flock, is another matter. And, mind, for the *man*
to be trust-worthy in this respect, the *boy* must have
been in the *habit* of being kind and considerate towards animals ; and nothing is so likely to give
him that excellent habit as his seeing, from his

very birth, animals taken great care of, and treated with great kindness, by his parents, and now-and-then having a little thing to *call* his *own*."

Yet, notwithstanding the protection thus afforded them by law, and the opinion thus expressed of their value, by one who had not the highest reverence for legislative wisdom, it is lamentable to think how much this poor persecuted emblem of innocence has been made to administer to the base and depraved propensities of some of the lower members of the modern sporting world.

Chalk Farm has risen into a new, and as little to be envied, notoriety, by men now shooting pigeons there, as fools, with a greater regard at least to justice, stood to shoot at one another, for the poor pigeon has less chance against a crack cockney shot, than the duellist against the hair-trigger of his antagonist. The trembling hand, or the leadless barrel of the latter, may insure safety, but dozens of pigeons, despite their power of wing, and speed of flight, are brought down merely for the settlement of some quarrelling bets, or as the prelude to some tavern dinner, or tavern brawl, or the formation of a new match, where the same degrading scenes are to be repeated over again. Let it not be said there is no more harm in shooting a pigeon, than in pulling its neck. In point of morality, they are wide as the poles asunder. In every act regard the agent's end, and in the latter we see but a fulfilment of the destinies of nature, but in the other the fostering of vice, the indulgence of cruelty, and an administration to the basest passions of mankind.

Our readers may have read much in the periodi-
cals of the day, of Battersea-fields, the chief theatre
of the sport of pigeon shooting. In the words well
expressed of a well-informed writer, " That few people, even those accustomed to reflect on animal suf-
ferings, are aware of those of the wretched town-
pigeon ; harassed about from its first quitting the
nest, through the rough hands of scores of unfeeling
blackguards ; its feathers pulled, its wings *braced*,
starved,and forced to fly against its inclination, matched, then unmatched, and its dearest ties broken ;
sold, resold, exposed in cages, immersed in cellars,
coal-holes, and loaded with every misery which can
be inflicted by the wanton caprice, neglect, and
beastly ignorance of the two-legged race, its tyrants."
British Field Sports.—It is better not to be initated
into the fancy pigeon " Cultivation" at all, or merely to keep pigeons for the use of the table, with the
additional pleasure to be derived from contemplating
their flight, with a degree of attention to those birds
which are of the largest size, and most beautiful appearance. The best authenticated Treatise on Domestic Pigeons, especially regarding the fancy varieties, was published by Barry of Fenchurch Street,
in 1765, containing also some very good descriptive
plates. That Treatise has been succeeded by Moore's
Columbarium, and some others, founded on their
authority.

6. *Economy of Pigeons.*—The only breeds worth
keeping, exclusive of the common sort, are *Tumblers*,
Horsemen, Carriers, Turtles, Dragoons, (commonly
called Dragons), and *Runts*—the latter both Spanish

and Leghorn, for their great size. As breeders, no
fancy pigeons will in general equal the common
dove-house kind, unless perhaps with great care and
attention.

The pigeon is monogamous; that is, the male attaches once, confines himself to one female, and the
attachment is reciprocal—the fidelity of the dove to
its mate being proverbial. Yet it will be often seen
that the most bitter hate and deadly hostility prevail
among them. One will at times assume the reins
of even worse than eastern despotism, and tyrannize
it over the rest with the utmost cruelty. Then all
the symptoms of innocence disappear; all the stand-
ards of peace are furled; persecution, anarchy, and
confusion, usurp their place. This often arises from
the intrusion of a stranger, for it should be remarked
that pigeons have a proud as well as a generally
peaceful disposition, or rather they have, when once
attached to it, so much of the *amor dormi* as resent-
fully to resist the intrusion of a stranger, to lay
aside for a season their peaceful nature, and to take
up arms in resistance of a foreign invasion. Sometimes the intruder—especially if a strong, old, illna-
tured cock—will either succeed in putting the whole
of the native residents to the rout, or at least in giving them no peace at home. In this he succeeds by
attacking them singly, as soon as one appears upon
the lighting board, or if he chance to reign for a moment there alone, by darting fiercely upon the first individual that appears upon an adjoining roof. Pigeons do not seem to be aware of the power of com-
bination, or to have learned the doctrine that union

is strength, or a couple attacking such a fellow conjointly would annihilate him at once. But in such a case the only resource of the owner is to look to the instant destruction of the intruder, and it is only pigeons possessed of such a character that we would ever wish to see consigned to the sportsmen of Chalk Farm and Battersea-fields.

Young pigeons are termed *squeakers*, and begin to breed about the age of six months, when properly managed. Their courtship, and the well known tone of voice in the cock, just then acquired and commencing, are indications of their approaching union. Nestlings, whilst fed by the cock and hen, are termed *squabs*, and are at that age sold and used for the table. The Dove-house pigeon is said to breed monthly, being well supplied with food, more particularly when the ground is bound by frost or covered with At any rate, it may be depended on, that pigeons of almost any healthy and well established variety, will breed eight or ten times in the year; whence it may be conceived how immense are the quantities which may be raised.

It is nevertheless with difficulty that entire credit can be given to the calculations with respect to the increase either of pigeons or rabbits—bringing to our remembrance, to compare small things with great, the earths of gold of the celebrated Doctor Price, which have been so greatly reduced in number and weight by subsequent doctors. But we cannot question the positive testimony of Stillingfleet, who asserts that fourteen thousand seven hundred and sixty pigeons were produced from one single pair, in the

course of four years. To class things of a similar
bearing together, it has been calculated (but by whom,
or on what practical ground, is not well known,)
that a single pair of rabbits may produce one million two hundred and seventy-four thousand eight
hundred and forty of their kind ! This is a question
however more speculative than practical, and any
one who commences with a couple of pairs, if they
once proceed successfully, will find the increase sufficiently great to satisfy any reasonable expectation,
and to answer all domestic purposes which they
are intended to serve.

7. *The Dove Cote.*—The first step towards pigeon-
keeping is undoubtedly to provide a commodious
place for their reception ; the next, to provide the
pigeons themselves. These will be bred in pairs,
but if not actually *matched*, pairs must be afterwards
taken for that purpose, that no time may be lost ;
indeed, they may be matched according to the fancy
of the keepers, for the purpose of varying the colours, or with any other view. But it is necessary
to give a caution on the subject of *old pigeons*, of
which a bargain may offer, since the difficulty of returning them is so great, indeed insuperable, without
the strictest vigilance. Nothing short of cutting or
pulling their wing, and confining them closely, perhaps until they have young to attach them to the
place, will be a security ; and even afterwards, they
have been known to take flight with the first use of
their wings, and leave their nests. Thence it is always preferable to purchase *Squeakars*, or such as
have not yet flown ; these being confined, in a short

time, well fed, and accustomed gradually to the surrounding scenery, before they have acquired sufficient strength of wing wherewith to lose themselves, will become perfectly domesticated.

The *Dove Cote*, or pigeon-loft, as to its situation or extent, will necessarily depend on convenience; one *general rule*, however, must be invariably observed—that every pair of pigeons have two holes, or rooms, to rest in. Without this indispensable convenience, there will be no security, but the prospect of constant confusion, breaking of eggs, and destruction of the young. Pigeons do well near dwellings, stables, bake-houses, granaries, brew houses or such offices: or their proper place is in the poultry court.

A dove cote is a good object situated upon an island, in the centre of a piece of water; indeed, such is a proper situation for aquatic poultry, and rabbits also; and may be rendered extremely beautiful and picturesque by planting, and a little simple, ornamental, and useful building. Where pigeons are kept in a room, some persons prefer making their nests upon the floor, to escape the danger of the young falling out; but in all probability, this is to guard against one risk, and incur a greater danger, particularly that of rats and other vermin.

The front of the pigeon-room, or cote, should, if possible, have a south-west aspect; and if a room be selected for the purpose, it is usual to break a hole in the roof of the building, as a passage for the pigeons, which can be closed at convenience. A platform is laid by the carpenter at the entrance, for the pigeons to alight and perch upon, with some kind of defence against cats, which will often depopulate a whole dove-house. *Cats* are yet necessary for the defence of the pigeons against rats and mice, as they will both destroy the birds and suck the eggs; thence cats of a known good breed should be trained up familiarly with the pigeons. Yet still, especially in towns, they are exposed to great danger from strange-cats, belonging to neighbours. These will often find their way to the best guarded and best constructed pigeon-loft, from a great distance, and by peculiar stratagems, to which their instinct naturally leads them. Even when situated on the top of a lofty house we have known a whole flock destroyed or scared for ever from the place in a single night. Unless the house is completely isolated, there is no security for the pigeons for a single night, however long danger may have been previously escaped. In such circumstances a box, fastened to the wall near a window, will afford the greatest security, and sufficient convenience both for observation, amusement, and profit.

White being a favourite colour with pigeons, the platform must be so painted, and their boxes also; and the paint renewed as often as necessary, as the whiter their abode is, it adds the more towards its being a guide to them in their flight homeward. A portion of lime and water may be sufficient to renovate whiteness.

Cleanliness is one of the first and most important considerations; the want of it will soon render the dove-cote a nuisance, and the birds, both young and old, will be so covered with vermin, and besmeared with their own excrement, that they can enjoy no health or comfort, and mortality is often so induced. Ours were daily cleaned ; thoroughly once a week, a tub standing at hand for the reception of the dung, the floor covered with sifted gravel, often renewed. Pigeons are exceedingly fond of water, and, having a prescience of rain, they will be waiting until after sun-set, and spreading forth their wings, as in anxiety to be refreshed by the coming shower. When they are confined in a room, a fresh supply of water should be allowed them every day ; it cools and refreshes, and assists them to keep their bodies clear from vermin.

Great caution is necessary with respect to the pigeons fighting, to which they are more prone than might be supposed ; and it leads often to the destruction of eggs or young, and driving the weakest away. The common barrel dove-cote needs no description however we will give a short sketch of it, for the benefit of our juvenile readers.

The common Barrel Dove-cote is erected on a light staff or pole, adapted to every situation in which it is desirable to keep pigeons for ordinary use. To return to the *room* or *loft*: the shelves should be placed sufficiently high, for security against vermin, a small ladder being a necessary appendage. The usual breadth of the shelves is about twenty inches, with the allowance of eighteen between shelf and shelf, which will be sufficient not to incommode the tallest pigeon. Partitions between the shelves may be fixed at the distance of about three feet, making

a blind, by a board nailed against the front of each
partition, whence there will be two nests in the compass of every three feet, so that the pigeons will sit
in privacy ; or a partition may be fixed between each
nest—a good plan, which prevents the young running to the hen, sitting over fresh eggs, and perhaps
occasioning her to cool and addle them ; for when
the young are about a fortnight or three weeks old,
a good hen will leave them to the care of the cock,
and lay again.   Some prefer *breeding holes,* entirely
open in front, for the greater convenience in clear-
ing the nests ; but it is from those that the *squabs*
are likely to fall, thence a step of sufficient height is
preferable.   The tame pigeon seldom taking the
trouble to make a nest, it is better to give her one
of hay, which prevents her eggs from rolling.   A basket, or an unglazed earthen pan, may be placed in
every nest, apportioned to the size of the pigeon you
breed.   A pan of three inches high, eight over the
top, and sloping towards the bottom like a basin,
will be sufficiently large for a *Tumbler,* whilst one of
double those dimensions will be required for a *Runt.*
A brick ought always to be placed near enough the
pan, to enable the cock and hen to alight with safety upon the eggs.   The *Pigeon-trap* on the house-top,
is the well known contrivance of those *London* ras-
cals who lie in wait to entrap the property of others.
A trap of another description, but for a very different purpose, is sometimes used ; it is an area, on the
outside of a building, for the purpose of confining
in open air, valuable braces of pigeons which cannot
be trusted to flight.   Some are erected to the extent

of twenty yards long, and ten yards in width, with shelves on every side, for the perching of the pigeons; thus they are constantly exercised in the air, retiring at pleasure to the room or loft within. Very convenient *baskets* are now made in the cradle form, with separate apartments, and serve for the carriage of pigeons, for matching, putting them up to fatten, or any other of the usual purposes. *Food and water* should be given in such a way as to be as little as possible contaminated with the excrement, or any other impurity. If pigeons are constantly attended to, there is no need of any other convenience than earthen pans; there have been ingenious inventions for this purpose, of which the *meat box* and *water bottle* following are specimens. The meat-box is formed in shape of a hopper, covered at top to keep clean the grain, which descends into a square shallow box. Some fence this with rails or holes on each side, to keep the grains from being scattered over; others leave it quite open, that the young pigeons may the more easily find their food. The *water-bottle* is made to contain from one to five gallons, it has a long neck, and a body shaped like an egg, so as to prevent the pigeons from lighting on it, and dunging it. It is placed upon a stand, made hollow above, to receive the bottle, and let the mouth into a small pan beneath: the water will, in such wise, gradually descend from the mouth of the bottle as the pigeons drink, be sweet and clean, and always stop when the surface reaches the mouth of the bottle.

8. *Matching, or Pairing and Breeding of Pigeons.*— To match or pair a cock and hen, it is necessary to

shut them up together, and within reach of each other; and the connexion is generally formed in a day
or two. Various rules have been laid down, by
which to distinguish the cock from the hen pigeon;
but the masculine forwardness and action of the cock
is, for the most part, distinguishable. *Incubation.*—
The great increase of domestic pigeons does not proceed from the number of eggs laid by them, but from
the frequency of their hatching. The hen lays but
two eggs, and immediately proceeds to incubation.
Having laid her first egg she rests one day, and on
the next lays her second one. They usually stand
over the first egg, not setting close until they have
two, whence both the young are hatched nearly at
the same time. There are some exceptions, however, to this rule of nature, and the hen having sat
close at first, one young bird may be hatched before
the other. They often spoil their first eggs from in-
experience. The *period* of *incubation* is nineteen or
twenty days from laying the first egg, and seventeen
or eighteen from the second. The duty of setting is
shared equally between the cock and hen, excepting
that the hen always sits by night. She is relieved in
the morning by the cock, which sits during the greater part of the day. The business of feeding the
young! is, also divided between the parents, and the
cock has often brought up the young, on the accidental loss of his mate. Should the eggs not be hatched
in due time, from weakness, some small assistance
may be necessary to extricate the bird from the
shell; or should they be addled, it is generally held
necessary to provide the cock and hen with a bor-

rowed pair of young ; or at least one, to feed off
their soft meat, which else may stagnate in their
crops, and make them sick ; but as young ones may
not always be at hand for this purpose, the exercise
of flying, fresh gravel, and those saline compositions
generally given to pigeons, are the proper remedies.
Addled, or rotten eggs should be immediately removed.   Pigeons are extremely liable to be lost by accident, and that which is unaccountable, although
they will find their home from such great distance,
they nevertheless often lose themselves in their own
neighbourhood.   Should a pair be lost during incubation, the eggs will spoil in twenty or thirty hours,
and may then be taken from the nest ; but if the accident happen after hatching, the parent left will
feed the young.   The young are easily accustomed
to be fed by the hand, should both parents happen to
be lost.   For this purpose barley should seldom be
tried, as tares and small peas are far preferable.   A
hollow reed through which the food should be squirt-
ed into their mouths, is an old practice, but more
honoured in the breach than in the observance.

That sort of milky fluid secreted in the crop of pigeons, during the latter period of the process of incubation, and commonly called *soft meat*, has been
wisely intended by the wisdom of Providence as a
suitable provision at the proper time for the nourishment of their young.   It is probable that at this
period the breeding pigeons eat a greater quantity of
food than is required for their own support, and what
does not pass through the digestive process is left in
the crop, where it softens, and is melted into a milky

6

pap. This at pleasure they have the power of throwing up, and in feeding, they inject it into the bills
of the young from their own, those of the young having been inserted into those of the old. This kind
of feeding continues six or seven days, when the old
ones begin to mix some harder food with it, until at
length they feed with whole grain. When the time
approaches for the hen to lay, the cock is often seen
driving her from place to place, not suffering her to
rest any where but in her nest, apparently from an
instinctive apprehension that she may drop her egg
in an improper place.

9. *Food of Pigeons.*—Pigeons are very cleanly in
their habits, and entirely granivorous in their diet.
Sometimes they will eat green vegetables, particularly warm salad, but are more particularly addicted to
dry and ripened grain, on which alone they can thrive
well and long. Tares, peas, and the smallest kind
of black or brown beans, commonly called pigeon
beans, are good, but as new pulse is apt to scour
them, as well as all other kinds of live stock, care
should be taken that they are completely dry, and of
the previous year's growth. As seeds are sometimes
given to pigeons, to warm and stimulate them, rape
or canary should always be preferred to hemp-seed,
and to the former, the pigeons themselves show a
decided preference. Beans sodden in salt water
have a tendency to scour pigeons as much as new
beans; and on a sea voyage, they will soon be killed
if permitted to drink salt water. Although they,
as well as vegetation, are so much profited by salt,
an excess of it is equally fatal to both.

The term applied to beans, is frequently misrepresented by writers, and mistaken by feeders. Small *tick* beans are recommended by the one and used by the other, instead of small horse-beans. Now the *tick* or *kidwell*, in the western phrase, are the larger of the two common field varieties, and besides being inferior in quality, are too large for pigeons, which have been sometimes choked even with the common-size horse beans; on which account the smallest possible should be procured, whence such are termed in the market accounts, "pigeon beans." Peas, wheat, and buck-wheat, or brank, are eaten by pigeons: but should be given only in alternations, not as their constant diet. Of seeds, the same may be said. Upon the olfactory nerves of pigeons, as also their palates, the strong scent of cumine and of asafœtida, with other odoriferous drugs, the flower of the coriander, and other seeds, have a powerful and alluring effect; to fumigate the dove-cot with these will not only attach the pigeons more strongly to home, but will also allure strangers that may be wandering about in search of a habitation.

The last dietetic, or rather, perhaps, medicinal article necessary to be described, is the SALT CAT, so called from some old fancy of baking a real cat with spices, for the use of pigeons, which, however, I never observed to eat animal food. In compliance with this custom, I caused to be placed in the middle of the pigeon-loft, a dish of the following composition : loam, sand, old mortar, fresh lime, bay-salt, cumine, coriander, carraway seed, and alspice, moistened into the consistence with urine. The pigeons were constantly picking at this, were in a constant state of good health: how much of which may be attributed to the use of the cat, I cannot determine ; but, certainly, they are extremely fond of it, and if it had no other merit, it prevents them from picking the mortar from the roof of the house, to which otherwise they are much inclined. The cat was mixed and heaped up in the dish, a piece of board being placed upon the summit, to prevent the birds from dunging upon it : when become too hard, it was occasionally broken for them.

The regular OLD FORMULA for this cat is as follows : gravel or drift-sand, unctuous loam, the rubbish of an old wall, or lime, a gallon of each—should lime be substituted for rubbish, a less quantity of the former will suffice—one pound of cumine-seed, one handful of bay salt ; mix with stale urine. Inclose this in jars, corked or stopped, holes being punched in the sides, to admit the beaks of the pigeons. These may be placed abroad.

10. *Uses of Pigeons.*—The pigeons must have been principally intended to form a part of the food of man. In health, it is to him a delicate luxury on his table and in sickness it sometimes forms his only diet when the heart loathes all else besides. In the olden times, numerous fanciful medicinal properties were assigned to the flesh of the pigeon. Almost every part of its body from head to rump had its peculiar and appropriate remedial function assigned to it ; and although all of this has been long and justly repudiated as old wives' fables, that the pigeon forms a *piquant* and nourishing diet, no one doubts. When

young and in good condition, they are tender to the palate of the infant, and stimulating to the appetite of the invalid, but when old, more heating and difficult of digestion, although more substantial and nourishing. The general rule that the colour of the plumage affects the qualities of the flesh, is peculiarly true of the pigeon. The blue and dark-feathered are proportionably tinged in the colour of their flesh, and are of high flavour, approaching to the game bitter of the wild pigeon. Light and delicate flesh is invariably associated with white and silvery colour of the feathers. Whether for manure or medical purposes, their excrements are of a peculiarly heating nature. When saltpetre was almost entirely manufactured at home, it formed a principal ingredient in the composition of nitre beds.

Although we have already incidentally taken notice of the flight of pigeons, and some of their achievements in this capacity, that subject seems to demand still more explicit notice here, as it has sometimes been made the means both of public and of private utility. Even the most common Carriers, Horsemen, Dragoons, and sometimes Tumblers, are thrown off at a distance of forty miles from home. This distance generally takes from an hour and a half to three hours, although in three successive hours a journey of ninety miles has been performed—an achievement to which no other animal known to man is equal, and which it is doubtful if either the power of steam or of any other agent will be ever able to surpass. A Dragoon has flown seventy-six miles in two hours and a half: this ancient fancy of flying pigeons had declined, but has, it seems, revived within a few years. The admired qualities in the Tumbler are excessive high flight, so as to be almost imperceptible to the keenest eye, in fine and clear weather, perseverance in their flight for many hours together, and tumbling over and over repeatedly du_ing their ascent and descent.

THE RABBIT.

RABBITS are delicate, tender, and cleanly creatures. In a state of nature they are active and hardy, living in the midst of apparent barrenness, and
requiring nothing for their support but what the
most stunted soil is able to afford. The wild rabbit
is almost invariably of a grey colour, and for the table is generally preferred to the best fed and most
beautiful varieties reared in the hutch. It bears
some striking analogies to the hare—although in its
habits and constitutional peculiarities it manifests as
striking diversities. To agricultural produce in the
neighbourhood of extensive preserves, they are found
to be very destructive, as they will often travel in
flocks to a considerable distance in search of food.
To farmers situated near a rabbit-warren they are a
great nuisance, as in their marauding excursions,
when they find the soil and corn to their liking, they
will settle down and speedily breed in sufficient
numbers to colonize a new district. Where there
are extensive wastes, downs covered with arid ver-
dure, sand, or rocky shores, the rabbit however becomes a valuable property. The march of improve-

ment has banished them from many of their wonted haunts in Scotland—streets and villas now rearing their heads on the very spot where the untamed cony used to burrow and to gambol. Within a few miles of Edinburgh, and that too in the course of a few years, the site of a rabbit-warren has been converted into a borough and a parliamentary town, whose natives, instead of being shot or snared, it has been the delight of two Lord Advocates of Scotland to represent in the British Senate—the glories of Rabbit-hall have been dimmed, and in vain are their haunts to be sought for, at Park-House or Pitt-Street.

1. *The Wild Rabbit.*—Those kept in a domesticated state are always larger, with more variegated colouring and peculiar points of conformation than the wild or warren rabbit. In some warrens a few black, black and white, and even fawn-coloured rabbits, are to be found, but the general colour is grey. The flesh of wild rabbits is more delicate, with more of the game flavour, and in general preferred to the tame. By judicious feeding, and affording the animals good air and sufficient room for exercise, the domesticated kinds may however be much improved in the firmness and flavour of the flesh.

The wild rabbit is said to breed eleven times in the year. This is possible, but not very probable. In general they produce eight young ones each time, and at this rate a couple of rabbits would produce in four years a progeny of nearly a million and a half. When domesticated, the rabbit is much more profitable than in a wild state, even with all this fecundity, for a prudent keeper will look more to the quality than to the number of the produce. Six or eight litters in the year is in general deemed sufficient. These by proper nursing will turn out to better account at the end of the year than the more numerous offspring of the wild rabbit. Many of the wild rabbits are destroyed by damp, by the buck, and by the numerous four-footed enemies to which they are exposed. In a state of nature they are the most defenceless of creatures, and if it were not for their prolific nature the whole race would speedily become extinct.

2. *Common Domestic Rabbits.*—Common domestic rabbits are of every variety of colour. Their prices depend upon their age, size, and beauty. In some parts of the east coast of England, they can be bought when young for two shillings a dozen, but in London they generally cost from a sixpence to a shilling each. The average value of a half grown or full grown rabbit of a large size is from half a crown to four shillings. In keeping common rabbits, one of the principal objects besides the amusement they afford to children is, to provide a dish for the table ; therefore those who trade in rabbits pay as much attention to the quality of the flesh as to the colour of the skin.

As to the varieties of form and colour in the rabbit, the short-legged, with width and substance of loin, generally few in number, and to be obtained only by selection, are the most hardy, and fatten most expeditiously, taking on fat both internally and in the muscular flesh. They have besides the soundest livers, rabbits being generally subject to defects of the liver, and they are the smallest variety. There was formerly a very large variety of the hare colour, having much bone, length and depth of carcase, large and long ears, with large eyes resembling those of the hare. They might well be takien for hybrid or mules, did not their breeding militate against the idea. Their flesh is high coloured, substantial, and more savoury than that of the common rabbit : and they make a good dish, cooked like the hare, which, at six or eight months old, they nearly equal in size. Of late years this large variety has become very scarce. The large white, and yellow and white species, have whiter and more delicate flesh, and cooked in the same way will rival the turkey.

With respect to colour, the wild colour and black are preferred, and the skins are of full as much value as the white. The Turkish or French rabbit, with long white fur, differs little from the common varieties ; nor are their skins of more value, either for sale or home use. The skins are sometimes dried for linings of light gowns and other domestic purposes ; but the short close fur is always found to be the best.

The *smut* is a mark of peculiar distinction in the rabbit. It is a spot on the nose, of which there are three varieties—the single, the double, and the butterfly smut. The darker the colour of these spots the more valuable is the animal deemed. According to the old fanciers they ought to be black, or at least of the darkest hue that the original exhibits on any part of its skin. The single smut is a patch of colour on one side of the nose—the double is a patch on each side—and the butterfly is 'a double smut, with a mark of the same colour running a little distance up the ridge of the nose in such a manner that the whole resembles a butterfly reversed, of which the two marks on the sides are the wings, and that on the front of the nose, body and tail. Such rabbits were at one time classed among the fancy ones, but they are now considered only a very fine kind of the domestic breed.

3. *Lop-eared or Fancy Rabbit.*—Rabbits are frequently divided into four kinds : warrens, parkers, hedgehogs, and sweethearts. Burrowing under ground is favourable to the growth of fur in them all, and the warren, though inhabiting a subterraneous residence, is less effeminate than his kindred who roam more at large. His fur is more esteemed, and after him comes the parker, whose favourite haunt is a gentleman's pleasure grounds, where he usually breeds in great numbers, and not unfrequently drives the hares away. The hedgehog is a sort of vagabond rabbit, who travels tinker-like throughout the country, and who would be better clad if he remained at home. Sweethearts are tame rabbits, and their fur, though sleek, is too silky and soft to be of much use in the important branch of hat-making.

There is a peculiar breed of Lincolnshire rabbits, styled the silver-tipped, having the fur of a dark or lighter grey, mixed with longer hairs tipped with white. Many of this description may be seen in the vicinity of the metropolis, where they were bred, without any knowledge in the breeders of their Lincolnshire origin. Their skins, of no extra value here, are said to be in demand for exportation to Russia and China, and thence bought up in large quantities by the fur merchants for exportation.

Formerly a fine animal of any two colours was considered a fancy rabbit, but now the character is confined to those possessed of long lopped ears. The graceful fall of the ears is the first thing that is looked to by the fancier, next the dew-lap, if the animal is in its prime, then the colours and marked points, and lastly, the shape and general appearance. The ears of a fine rabbit should extend not less than seven inches, measured from tip to tip, in a line across the skull, but even though they should exceed this length, they are admitted with reluctance into a first-rate fancy stock, unless they have a uniform and graceful droop. The dewlap is only seen in fancy rabbits after they have attained their full growth; it commences immediately under the jaw, and adds much to the beauty of their appearance. It goes down the throat, and between the forelegs, and is so broad, that it projects beyond the chin, when the head reposes on it. A very fine effect is produced by it, when the fur with which it is clothed is of a beautiful colour. The difference between the fancy and the common rabbit in the back and general appearance, independently of the ears, is sufficient to strike the most common observer.

Fancy rabbits cost a very high price, so much as five, ten, and even twenty guineas having been given for a first-rate doe. If young ones are first procured of a good lineage, the foundation of an excellent stock can be laid for a much smaller sum, and by judicious pairing and crossing, some splendid varieties may at times be produced. Very excellent specimens have occasionally been thrown off by those who have good blood in their veins, although they themselves should not be perfect, but even exhibit some inferior points. The original pairs should, in this case, be got rid of as soon as possible, and the best models for future breeding retained. By this means, he who begins with a cheap, and even an inferior stock, may soon come to enter into successful competition with one who commenced with the purest and highest priced kinds.

Sometimes the ears, instead of drooping down, slope backwards. A rabbit with this characteristic is scarcely admitted into the fancy catalogue, and is not considered worth much more than the common variety. The next and most general position of the ears, is when one lops outward, and the other stands erect. Rabbits of this kind possess little value, however fine in shape, and beautiful in colour, although they sometimes throw off as good specimens as those which are quite perfect. Though only one-half lop-up-eared, they are in general fully bred, and as a consequence, their progeny is often superior to themselves.

The *forward* or *horn lop* is one degree nearer perfection than the half lop. The ears in this case slope forward and down over the forehead. Rabbits with this peculiarity are sometimes perfect in all other respects, with the exception of the droop in the ears, and often become the progenitors of an illustrious posterity, purified from all their imperfections, and possessed of all their excellencies. Does of this kind frequently have the power of lifting one ear upright.

In the *ear top*, the ears spread out in a horizontal position, like the wings of a bird in flight, or the arms of a man in swimming. A great many excellent does have this characteristic, and some of the best bred bucks in the fancy are entirely so. Sometimes a rabbit drops one ear completely, but raises the other so nearly horizontally as to constitute it an ear top : this is superior to all others except the perfect fall, which is so rarely to be met with, that those which are merely ear topped are considered very valuable animals, if well bred, and with other good qualities.

The *real top* has ears that hang down by the side of the cheek, slanting somewhat outward in their descent with the auricular parts inward, and sometimes either backward or forward instead of perpendicular. When the animal stands in an easy position, the tips of the ears touch the ground. The hollows of the ears in a fancy rabbit of the first rate kind, should be turned so completely backward, that only the outer or convex part of them may appear in front. They should match exactly in their descent, and should slant outward as little as possible. Perfectly handsome lops are considered so rare, that a breeder with a stock of twenty does of the most capital kind, with superior blood and beauty, may think himself fortunate if he can get a dozen full lopped ears, in the course of a year, out of them all,

4. *Colour of Rabbits.*—As the common rabbit is

reared principally for the table, weight and size are with it more important requisites than colour, both for culinary and other economical purposes, as well as taste. Sometimes indeed a stock of rabbits has been kept almost entirely for their skins.

The old writers perhaps rather overvalued the profits of this stock. Rabbit-keeping is practised by a few individuals in almost every town, and by a few in almost every part of the country; but thirty or forty years ago, there were one or two very considerable feeders near the metropolis, keeping each, according to report, from fifteen hundred to two thousand breeding does. These large concerns have ceased, it seems, long since, and London receives the supply of tame, as well as wild rabbits, chiefly from the country.

The most considerable rabbit-feeders in England some years ago, were two gentlemen, the one resident in Oxfordshire, the other in Berks. The former fed some hundreds, and then, it was said, intended to double his stock. The huts were placed in a small building set apart for that purpose. The then stock produced one load of dung per week, two loads of which were sufficient to manure an acre of land. Three dozen of rabbits per week were sent to the London market, but keep and attendance reckoned, no other profit accrued, excepting the dung, the price of which used to be eight-pence per bushel, and I believe thirty-six bushels are reckoned a load. The Berks gentleman, according to the survey of that county, fed white rabbits, on account of the superior value of their skins, from their application of late years to the purpose of trimmings. Twenty does and two bucks will form a large stock.

Tortoise shell (a rich brown and white, and brown grey and white) as also jet black, and pure white, are reckoned the best colours by fanciers. Mouse colour is much admired by a chosen few. Fawn, and fawn and white, and grey, have also their admirers. The cook, however, has peculiar delight in the grey and the black ; they are of a hardy constitution, form good breeders, and are capital eating.

Fanciers attach much importance to the manner in which the colours are mixed. The greater part of the back, the haunches, and the body, should be of the dark hue, or slightly spotted with the lighter hue. A chain, or series of the darker colour, should come up to the shoulders, and the rest of the fore part of the body should also be variegated—white, however, predominating. If the ears are of not precisely the prevailing colour of the body, they are called pie-bald, which is considered a great defect. A great deal of colour, not unmingled with white, should surround the eyes, and cover the nose. The throat and dewlap may be either white, dark, or variegated, and the belly altogether white. There should be as few white hairs as possible on any of the spots or dark parts, especially those of the back, for they make the animal appear grizzled and deficient in beauty. The spots should be distinctly defined on the white ground. When the colour on the back gradually melts away into the white by an intermixture of white hairs, instead of being gradually and clearly broken by distinct edges and terminating with the chain on the shoulders, the animal is always considered deteriorated. The rabbits, however, that are perfectly coloured, are extremely few, and they only approach perfection the more closely they coincide with the description we have thus given.

All the rabbits in the fancy stock that do not appear improving upon the colour of their progenitors, should be consigned to the cook. They should be condemned to feast the palate, when they are not fit to please the eye, and it is always better to have a select than merely a numerous assortment. When rabbits from first-rate does exhibit this deterioration of colour, they are called blood-suckers, because they impoverish the stock, by taking the food and milk which might nourish a more esteemed brood. The thorough rabbit-fancier never thinks of rearing merely for the table. It is his object and his interest to sell them to those of a taste similar to his own, but if he keeps a number of does he is under the necessity of weeding his stock by devoting them to his own use, or taking the regular market price for them from the poulterer, as out of every score which he may think it proper, on account of their colours, to rear to the age of two months, three-fourths of them will be found of no value from defect in their ears. He is too knowing, however, to send them out of his hands alive, as this would give others an opportunity of raising a comparatively valuable stock, though of an inferior grade, which would tend to lower prices in the fancy market. There is a story told of a pigeon-fancier who was offered a guinea for a pair for which he had asked five times the amount, having

7

wrung off their heads to provide for his supper ; and it is also said that a poulterer had concluded a bargain with a person who kept good rabbits, for a lot of young ones, at half-a-crown a pair, and when he proposed taking them home alive, he was told, that in that case they must cost a guinea. The reason is obvious. Although the present generation might appear imperfect, and not worth the keeping to the eye of the fancier, some of their posterity might turn out well, and the excellences of the original stock might thus be transferred to the possession of a stranger who had not paid any thing like an adequate price.

Fine coloured rabbits should never be sacrificed on account of any defect in their ears, as they are sometimes known to throw off beautiful loppers, and to become the founders of an excellent family ; whereas, those with drooping ears, but of mean colour, and of puny form, frequently give rise to a paltry erect-eared race. It is a mistake to keep them on account of their ears alone, fine points and beautiful colour being of far greater importance. It is equally foolish, and withal a cruel practice, to cause the ear to droop by artificial means. Unless it be to serve some purpose of jockey-ship, it is labour in vain, and seldom followed even with the appearance of temporary success. It is better to attend principally to the colour and general constitution, leaving lopped-eared progeny to the chapter of accidents, as more or less of them will be turned out in the ordinary and regular increase of the stock.

5. *The Rabbit Hutch.*—The great requisite in a

rabbitry, whether large or small, is dryness and fresh air; the want of either of which is equally destructive to the inmates. In securing free ventilation, every precaution should be used to prevent strong and irregular currents of air, which pras injurious to the health as a confined and humid us atmosphe, and is apt to bring on a disease called the snuffles, a dangerous and fatal disorder. The young fancier should attend more to the situation in which his hutches are placed, than to the materials of which they are composed. He should, if possible, choose the summit of a sloping bank on a dry and sandy soil. The floor of the hutch should be an inclined plane, with a small opening at the bottom to carry off any superfluous moisture. It should always be divided into two compartments, the outer one railed in, and only half covered with a hinged rail on the uncovered part, which can be opened at pleasure for the purpose of inspection or feeding. The inner apartment should have the whole of the lowe inwall on hinges, that it may be thoroughly and regularly cleaned. In the corner of a small park, or green, or garden, such a hutch can easily be constructed, by any active youth, with a few old boards, at almost no expense. We do not approve of old tea-chests or egg boxes, unless for the purpose of temporary confinement or separation, and a few of these may always be at hand for managing the progress of the breeding stock. It is preferable to rest the hutches upon stands, about a foot above the ground, for the convenience of cleaning under them. Each of the hutches, intended for breeding, should have two rooms, a feeding and

a bed room. Those are single for the use of the
WEANED RABBITS, or for the BUCKS, which are always,
except at the proper season, kept separate.

When much green meat is given, rabbits make
a considerable quantity of urine, and I have sometimes seen occasion to set the hutches sloping backwards a few degrees. a very small aperture being
made the whole length of the floor, to carry off the
urine. A sliding door in the partition between the
two rooms is convenient for confining the rabbits
during the operation of cleaning ; which, indeed, is
a good argument for having all the hutches double,
it being more troublesome to clean out a room with
a number of rabbits in it, than with only one. It
must not be forgotten, that the teeth of rabbits are
very effectual implements of destruction to any thing
not hard enough to resist them, and their troughs
should be bound with something less penetrable than
wood. As they are apt to scratch out their food
and dung into it, I have often thought it might be
useful to adopt the feeding troughs with moveable
boards, as well for rabbits as for pigs.

The floor of the hutches should be planed smooth,
that wet may run off, and a common hoe with a short
handle, and a short broom, are most convenient implements for cleaning these houses. The hutches
should be littered with refuse hay or straw, perfectly dry. The rabbit-house should contain a tub for
the dung, and a bin for a day's supply of hay, corn,
roots, or other food, which should be given in as
fresh a state as possible.

There are other modes of confining rabbits for

breeding, in which they are left to their liberty, with-in certain bounds: for example, an artificial mound walled in, in which they burrow and live as in the natural state, and an island, as described in Mr. Young's Annals,—methods which are certainly or-namental and pleasurable, and more perhaps for the comfort of the animals; but not so profitable to the owner as hutching, in which mode also they may be preserved, with due care, in the highest state of health. "On this head," says Mowbray, "I find the following remark in my memoranda for the year 1805: *Rabbits at large must always suffer more in point of profit, by loss of number, than they gain, by cheaper feeding, ex-clusive of the mischief they do:* and this principle operates proportionally in limited enlargement, as in the unlimited upon the warren. They are quarrel-some and mischievous animals, and the bucks when at liberty destroy a considerable part of the young. A run abroad indeed for young rabbits, until a cer-tain age, might be beneficial if *growth* were the sub-ject; but all rabbits must be separated at the age of puberty, or as soon as they become fit for breeding; they will else tear each other to pieces."

With all due deference we must beg leave to dif-fer from this respectable authority, as we have found from experience that the more the common rabbit, and even some approaching to a fine fancy breed, are allowed to run and gambol in the open air, the har-dier, healthier, and more prolific they become, re-quiring less attention, and in every respect afford-ing more pleasure and profit to the keeper. When there is convenience for it, a small enclosed unpaved court on a sandy substratum, dry and firm, of about twelve or twenty feet square, or oblong of such dimensions, is one of the best little domestic warrens that can be formed, giving the animals all the advantages of a state of nature and a state of domestication at the same time. Here they will frisk and burrow, bringing forth their young safe from the ravages of the buck and every enemy, and the litter is seldom seen till,—when the young are about a month old,—they emerge from their subterraneous bed, and run about like little living snowballs. When thus brought up they are apt to become a little wild, but hunger is the great tamer of all animated being, and the necessity they are under of returning to the hutch for food, soon accustoms them to the presence, and subjects them to the hand of man. It is objected to this mode of training, that the burrowing of the rabbits is apt to undermine, and one worthy guardian of ours, when we first adopted the process, felt serious alarm lest the whole house should tumble down about his ears. But this is altogether a mistake, as the burrow of the rabbit forms a strong arch, and any thing placed upon it stands as securely as on the solid ground. On the banks of the Firth of Forth we once enjoyed a situation of this kind, and neither before nor since have we ever enjoyed so much satisfaction in the rearing of rabbits. They defied all the attacks of cat, or dog, and weasel, even when the gate at the bottom of their hutch was left open for days and nights; and it would eventually have required a keen ferret to have scented them out of their many lurking places.

For fancy rabbits, however, distinct hutches are necessary. They should be boxes placed against the wall, and raised from the ground, with wire fronts. They should have drawers in the front for food, and moveable bottoms for cleaning, something on the same principle as a bird cage. The hutch of the doe should be divided by a partition, with a small sliding door in it. She should never be allowed to feed in the inner or breeding division, and both should be kept thoroughly dry and clean. It is unnecessary to have any partition in the buck's hutches. They should be of a semicircular form, with the chord at the front, from which the sides and back should be gradually rounded off. The wires are placed wide apart, and are stronger and thicker than those used for does' hutches, The drawer is placed in the centre, as there is only one to feed, instead of running the whole length of the front. The buck's hutch should not be less than twenty inches high, thirty broad, and twenty at its deepest part.

The hutches may be placed one above the other, or placed in a row as circumstances may permit, or choice direct. If possible they should never stand on the ground, but on stools or horses about a foot or two high. The backs are better a little removed from the wall, and sufficient room should be left for the dung to have a passage through the openings made in the lower part of the floor.

6. *Feeding.*—Too much attention cannot be paid to this part of the subject, as it is upon his skill and attention in feeding, the greater part of the success and satisfaction of the young fancier will depend.

"*Abundant food*," says Cobbet, " is the main thing ; and what is there that a rabbit will *not eat* ? I know of nothing *green* that they will not eat ; and if hard pushed, they will eat bark, and even wood. The best thing to feed the young ones on when taken from the mother, is the *carrot*, wild or garden. Parsnips, Swedish turnips, roots of dandelion ; for too much green or *watery* stuff is not good for *weaning* rabbits. They should remain as long as possible with the mother. They should have oats once a-day ; and, after a time, they may eat anything with safety. But if you give them too much *green* at first when they are weaned, they *rot* as sheep do. A *variety* of food is a great thing ; and, surely, the fields and gardens and hedges furnish this variety ! All sorts of grasses, strawberry-leaves, ivy, dandelions, the *hog-weed or wild parsnip,* in root, stem, and leaves. I have fed working horses, six or eight in number, upon this plant for weeks together. It is a tall bold plant that grows in prodigious quantities in the hedges and coppices in some parts of England. It is the *perennial parsnip.* It has flower and seed precisely like those of the parsnip ; and hogs, cows, and horses, are equally fond of it. Many a half-starved pig have I seen within a few yards of cartloads of this pig meat ! This arises from want of the early habit of attention to such matters. I, who used to get hog-weed for pigs and for rabbits when a little chap, have never forgotten that the wild parsnip is good for pigs and rabbits.

When the doe has young ones, feed her most abundantly with all sorts of greens and herbage, and with carrots and the other things mentioned before, besides giving her a few oats once a day. The young ones, if they come from the mother in good case, will very seldom die. But do not think, that because she is a small animal, a little feeding is sufficient! Rabbits eat a great deal more than cows or sheep, in proportion to their bulk.

Of all animals rabbits are those that *boys* are most fond of. They are extremely pretty, nimble in their movements, engaging in their attitudes, and always completely under immediate control. The produce has not long to be waited for. In short, they keep an interest constantly alive in a little chap's mind; and they really *cost nothing*; for as to the *oats*, where is the boy that cannot, in harvest-time, pick up enough along the *lanes* to serve his rabbits for a year. The *care* is all; and the habit of taking care of things is, of itself, a most valuable possession.

To those gentlemen who keep rabbits for the use of their family (and a very useful and convenient article they are), I would observe, that when they find their rabbits die, they may depend on it, that ninety-nine times out of a hundred *starvation* is the malady. And particularly short feeding of the doe, while, and before she has young ones; that is to say, short feeding of her *at all times*; for if she be poor, the young ones will be good for nothing. She will *live* being poor, but she will not and cannot breed up fine young ones."

Too much food at a time is as bad as too little. It should be given often and in small quantities, fresh

and clean, that it may not litter and become putrid,
producing in the rabbit disgust and disease. Three
times a day is sufficiently frequent for all ordinary
purposes. In the morning to a full grown doe, with
no young to suckle, there should be given a little hay
dry, clean and green vegetables; at noon, two hand-
fuls of good corn should be put into her trough ; and
at night, a boiled potato or two, with a little more
hay or clover, but only if her hutch be quite clear of
what she got in the morning. The hay is trodden
down and wasted if more is given to them than they
are able to consume in a few hours, unless it be to
a doe just about to litter. It is eaten and relished
when but a moderate quantity is given to them at a
time. Green or moist food is generally preferred to
corn, but to keep them in health it is necessary to
furnish them with a regular supply of solid food.
A few split or grey peas may occasionally be given
them instead of corn. The peas may be soaked
a little before being put into the trough when intended for a doe, with a litter by her side, or for young
ones recently weaned. If a doe will not eat corn, a
few tea leaves may be mixed in her mess, and she
should be proportionably stinted in green food. To
gather for the table, or to bring a lean one into
good condition, barley meal, either dry or scalded, is
an excellent diet. Tea leaves may occasionally be
given them as a luxury, but never as their staple fare.

A doe will eat nearly double the quantity when
suckling that she will do at any other time, and
when her litter begin to eat, the allowance of food
should be gradually augmented. Sometimes when

afflicted with thirst, an extra portion of green food may be allowed, or some moistened grain, or even a spoonful of water, milk, or beer, but it is dangerous to expose them to moisture, either internally or externally.

7. *Breeding*.—The doe will breed at the age of six months, and her period of gestation is thirty or thirty-one days. It should be premised, that the buck and doe are by no means to be left long together; but their union having been successful, the buck must be inmediately withdrawn, and the doe tried again three days. Like chickens, the best breeding rabbits are those kindled in March. Some days before parturition, or kindling, hay is to be given to the doe, to assist in making her bed, with the flue which nature has instructed her to tear from her body for that purpose. She will be at this period seen sitting upon her haunches, and tearing off the flue, and the hay being presented to her she will with her teeth reduce and shorten it to her purpose. Biting down of the litter or bed, is the first sign of approaching delivery. The number produced is generally between five and ten; and it is most advantageous always to destroy the weak and sickly ones, as soon as their defects can be perceived, because five healthy and well-grown rabbits are worth more than double the number of an opposite description, and the doe will be far less-exhausted. She will admit the buck again with profit at the end of six weeks, when the young may be separated from her and weaned. Or the young may be suckled two months, the doe taking the buck at the end of five

weeks, so that the former litter will leave her about a week before her next parturition. A notion was formerly prevalent, of the necessity for giving the buck to the doe immediately after she had brought forth, lest she should pine, and that no time might be lost, but this is an unwise and unnatural practice, leading to the injury of health, and often to the loss of life. Great care should be taken that the doe during the period of her gestation be not approached by the buck, or indeed by any other rabbit ; as, from being harrassed about, she will almost certainly cast her young. One doe in a thousand may devour her young ; the sign that she ought to be otherwise disposed of. Some does admit the buck with difficulty, although often apparently in season ; such should be immediately fattened off, since it never can be worth while to keep an objectionable individual for breeding, of a stock to be produced in such multitudes. Should the doe be weak on her bringing forth, from cold caught, or other cause, she will drink beer-caudle, as well as any other lady ; or warm fresh grains will comfort her ; a malt mash, scalded fine pollard, or barley-meal, in which may be mixed a small quantity of cordial horse-ball.

Mr. Brown, of Banbury, who has published some observations on the subject, believes that what appears to be a propensity in the devouring her young, is nothing more than a necessitous, though truly unnatural act.

Mr. B. observes, " I have had rabbits which have been sold me cheap, in consequence of this seeming proneness to eat their young, which I have entirely

avoided by allowing the animal some short time
anterior, at the time, and for a week or so after parturition, to drink freely of cold water ; and when I
had taken this precaution, no such propensity ever
evinced itself in the least ; and that cold water is in
no way injurious and the animal appears wonder-
fully gratified by it.

"The preceding remarks go to prove, that the
propensity is in fact one which has necessity for its
origin ; and that of the most imperious nature.
Hence it is recommended to all who may have
suffered from this cause to supply the parturient
animals with as much cold liquid as they require
or can drink."

However plausible this theory of Mr. Brown may
be, and however occasionally useful, it must not be
received as generally correct. We must look deeper
than thirst, and the mere want of drink for the real
exciting cause of this apparently unnatural, perhaps
inscrutable act in females of various genera of
animals, since it is well-known to take place when
there is no such want, particularly in the rabbit, the
least liable to thirst, the sow, the cat, the ferret, and
others. The cow also devours her after-burden, in a
field of grass, and in reach of the pond at which she
is daily accustomed to drink. There are, moreover
formidable objections to this hypothesis of Mr.
Brown ; no light one in the solidity of the substanc,
chosen to allay thirst, better calculated, one would
suppose, to appease hunger ; and another weighty
one in the fact, that some, or most females, never
devour their young, under whatever circumstances

of privation. The doe will sometimes commit the act from resentment at having her bed and young disturbed and pried into, and will frequently tear her bed in pieces, and scatter the fragments about her hut.

Professor Coleman, in a very fanciful theory, attributes this unnatural practice in the doe to a consciousness of a deficiency in milk; but we consider that the above observations give a more rational and probable account of the matter.

Every litter should be reduced to five or six, by destroying the weak and sickly ones. Should the doe be weak after kindling, she should get a malt mash, scalded pollard or barley meal, in which may be mixed a small quantity of cordial horse-ball. In this or any other case in which a doe is weak, a little bread soaked in milk, and pressed dry again, may be given with great advantage. It is advisable to manage so as to make two or three does kindle at the same time, so that some of the young of the doe that has too many, may be transferred to the one that has too few, but never consigning more than six to each. In selecting for a breeding stock, the members of a small family should always be fixed as most likely to produce a vigorous and beautiful p rogeny.

8. *Diseases.*—Diseases may, in a great measure, be prevented by regularity in feeding, good food, and cleanliness. The refuse of vegetables should always be carefully rejected and removed. For the liver complaint there is no remedy, and when rabbits are affected with it, to which they are very liable, the only resource is to fatten them for the table. The

snuffles are brought on by damp and cold, and can only be cured, when cure is possible, by the opposite of that which caused it. They are sometimes infected with an ulcerous scab, which appears to be contagious, and the only course to be pursued is the separation of the sound from the tainted, as for the latter there is little or no hope.

Tea leaves are the most medicinal food that can be given when their health appears at all affected from any cause, but of all animals with which we are acquainted, the rabbit is the least able to resist the attack of disease, and seems the most to defy all medical and surgical skill. The grand object of attention should therefore be, to preserve them in health, which is seldom, if ever, a task of much difficulty.

9. *General Observations.*—With due attention to keeping them warm and comfortable, and guarding against any sudden impression from cold, and more particularly moist air, and with the aid of the best and most nourishing food, rabbits may be bred throughout the winter, with nearly equal success as in the summer season. But, in truth, their produce is so multitudinous, that one might be well satisfied with four or five litters, during the best part of the year, giving the doe a winter fallow. Even four litters would, upon the lowest calculation, produce twenty young ones annually to each doe; equal to an annual two thousand from a stock of one hundred does. Breeders have no experience of does beyond the fifth year, but the buck comes into use at six, or even four months old, and is in perfection from the age of two to three years.

Rabbits are generally sold from the teat, but there is also a demand for those of larger size, which may be fattened upon corn and hay with an allowance of the best vegetables. *The better the food, the greater weight, better quality, and more profit,* as is indeed the case in the breeding of all animals. Some fatten with fresh grains and pollard. Wheat, and all kinds of oats, have been tried comparatively, but little difference in the goodness of flesh has been found. The Rabbit's flesh being dry, the allowance of succulent greens may tend to render it more juicy. Rabbits are in perfection for feeding at the fourth or sixth month; beyond which period, their flesh becomes more dry and somewhat hard. It requires three months, or nearly so, to make a rabbit thoroughly fat and ripe; half the time may make them eatable, but by no means equal in the quality of the flesh. They may yet be over-fattened as appears by specimens exhibited a few years since, at Lord Somerville's show, a pair of which were loaded with fat without and within, like the highest fed sheep; and at the late London cattle show, two were exhibited, one of them exceeding the weight of 15 lbs.

The flesh of the rabbit is esteemed equally digestible with that of fowls, and equally proper for the table of the invalid. This seems to be the general sentiment, especially with regard to the sucking rabbit *boiled.* There is, nevertheless, some discrepancy of judgment between our sages of the table, as to the preference due to the wild or tame rabbit. In our opinion, the flesh of the wild rabbit is most savoury and substantial, that of the tame and home-fed, most delicate and chicken-like. We frequently observe a deep yellow suffusion, tinging the whole flesh and fat of the rabbit, and the same also in the turkey and in beef. It is difficult to conjecture or obtain any satisfactory reason for this phenomenon. Is the cause biliary? Of the two rabbits at the late show, one was white as silver, and the other a deep yellow, yet apparently both equally healthy.

Castrated rabbits might be fattened, no doubt, to the weight of upwards of ten or even fifteen pounds, at six or seven months old. The operation should be performed at the age of six or seven weeks. I have not succeeded at castrating the rabbit, but am informed it is successfully practised in that region of corn and capons, namely, Chichester in Sussex, where, on the average, not one in three hundred is lost by the operation, which is performed at five or six weeks old. With respect to quantities of corn consumed in fattening, Mowbray says, "August 1813, killed a young buck, which weighed three pounds, fit for the spit; it was put up in good case, and was only one month in feeding, consuming not quite four quarts of oats, with hay, cabbage, lucerne, *bunias orientalis*, and chicory; the skin, silver and black, worth four-pence."

In slaughtering full-grown rabbits, after the usual stroke upon the neck, the throat should be perforated upwards towards the jaws with a small pointed knife, in order that the blood may be evacuated, which would otherwise settle in the head and neck. It is an abomination to kill poultry by the slow and torturing method of bleeding to death, hung up by

8

the heels, the veins of the mouth being cut; but still more so the rabbit, which in that situation utters horrible screams. The entrails of the rabbits, whilst fresh, are said to be good food for fish, being thrown into ponds.

The rabbit is a caressing animal, and equally fond with the cat, of the head being stroked; at the same time it is not destitute of courage. A whimsical lady admitted a buck rabbit, named Corney Butter-cup, into the house, where he became her companion for upwards of a twelvemonth. He soon intimidated the largest cats so much, by chasing them round the room, and darting upon them, and tearing off their hair by mouthfuls, that they very seldom dared to approach. He slept in the lap by choice, or upon a chair, or the hearth-rug, and was as full of mischief and tricks as a monkey. He destroyed all rush-bottomed chairs within his reach, and would refuse nothing to eat or drink, which was eaten or drank by any other member of the family.

No live stock is less liable to disease than the rabbit, with regular and careful attention, such as has been pointed out, so that any sudden and accidental disorder is best and most cheaply remedied by a stroke behind the ears. But want of care must be remedied, if at all, by an opposite conduct, and improper food exchanged for its contrary. Thus if rabbits become pot-bellied in the common phrase, from being fed on loose vegetable trash, they must be cured by good hard hay and corn, ground malt or pease, toasted bread or captain's biscuits, or any substantial and absorbent food. Their common liver complaints are incurable, and when such are put up to fatten, there is a certain criterion to be observed. They will not bear to be pushed beyond a moderate degree of fatness, and should be taken in time, as they are liable to drop off suddenly. The dropsy and rot must be prevented, as they are generally incurable; nor is a rabbit worth the time and pains of a probable cure. Of the 'madness in tame conies,' on which our old writers hold forth, I know nothing.

Large rabbit concerns have now generally ceased; of late one has arisen at Ampthill, Bedfordshire, upon a more extensive scale than ever before attempted, established by J. H. Fisher, Esq. an agent of his Grace the Duke of Bedford. Upon so extensive a plan, indeed, is this new undertaking, that it may well be styled a grand NATIONAL RABBIT BAZAAR. The building situated upon an eminence is square, somewhat resembling barracks, with a court within-side the walls, and with thirty acres of fine light land adjoining, under culture of those crops known to be best adapted to the nourishment and support of four and five thousand breeding does, which number is probably now complete. The young rabbits, from seven to nine weeks old, are sent to Newgate and Leadenhall markets, fifty to sixty dozen weekly. The quantity of dung produced, which is preserved with the utmost care, and free from any extraneous substances, must be very considerable and valuable. A number of men and boys are employed in the concern, under the direction of an experienced foreman, and the utmost regularity of attention observed with respect to management, feeding, and cleanliness.

The above particulars are *memorable*, although this great undertaking came to an end in 1833, like so many former ones of a similar nature, but on a far inferior scale. Mr. Fisher probably found, though somewhat too late, that his other great concerns were fully sufficient to engage the whole of his attention. Experienced persons say, that the expenses necessarily attendant on such a concern were too heavy to admit of an adequate return of profit, one material item of which consisted in the too great distance of Ampthill from the metropolis. Nevertheless, it appears that three gentlemen were about to continue this undertaking on a smaller scale, at or near Shepherd's Bush.

THE CANARY BIRD.

——

1. *Origin.*—The canary bird belongs to the tribe Fringilla or Finch, and is chiefly found in a wild state among those islands of the Atlantic whence it derives its name. Its prevailing colour is yellow, though there is a second extensive variety with brown body and yellow eye-brows. Other varieties, or rather sub-varieties, have been described to the number of thirty, arising, doubtless, from domestication, and admixture with other Finches. It is about the size of a goldfinch. According to a late ornithologist, the second variety inhabits Africa, and it is said St. Helena, where it sings much better than the common canary in cages in this country. It is also found at Palma, Fayal, Cape Verd and Madeira, as well as at the Canaries. It is not known at what precise period it was introduced into Europe, but in all probability it could not be earlier than the fourteenth century. It is not mentioned by Below in the sixteenth century, and at the time of Gesner and Aldrovandus, who wrote his book upon birds at the beginning of the seventeenth century, it was considered a great rarity, and it was only to be met with in the mansions of the great.

The demand for them is now extensive ; they are bred and reared with facility under almost any circumstances, and the beauty of their plumage, with the melody of their song and the docility of their habits, have rendered them universal favourites. It is now thoroughly domesticated, and under cover almost completely naturalized throughout the whole of Europe. In South Western Germany and the Tyrol, their propagation has been converted into a trade, and is carried on by means of both extensive and expensive apparatus. A large building is erected for them, with a square space at each end, and holes communicating with these spaces. In these outlets are planted such trees as the birds prefer ; the bottom is strewed with sand and gravel, on which are thrown hemp-seed, rape-seed, chickweed, groundsel, &c. and such other food as the birds like. Throughout the inner compartment, which is kept dark, are placed brooms and young fir-trees, for the birds to build in,—care being taken that the breeding birds are guarded from the intrusion of the rest. Four Tyrolese usually take over to England about sixteen hundred of these birds ; although they carry them on their backs nearly a thousand miles, and pay £20 for them originally, they can sell them at 5s. each.

Some suppose that the note of the tame canary bird is compounded of that of the tit-lark and the nightingale. "But," observes Mr. Jennings, in his *Ornithologia*, "although this may be occasionally true, it is not, I suspect, a general truth. There is surely a probability that the canary has a song of its own." Of the eggs and incubation of this bird in its natural state, it is equally difficult to obtain any account. "In its domestic state," says Mr. Jennings, "it doubtless partakes of the nature of those birds with which it might happen to be associated." Mr. Yarrel, however, communicated to Mr. Jennings' work the following particulars of the domesticated canary bird, of which he (Mr. Yarrel) has several eggs, produced by the genuine species, without any admixture.

"Whatever the materials are of which the canary forms its nest, or what the colour of its eggs in its native islands, I do not know; but in this country, (having bred them myself,) they make a compact nest of moss and wool, closely interwoven, very similar to the nest of the linnet and the red-pole; the egg is also very like that of the linnet, but some-what smaller; the ground colour white, slightly tinged with green, spotted and streaked, with dark red at the larger end; in number, four or five.

"However domestication may change the feather, I have no reason to believe that it produces any alteration in the colour of the egg, and in this instance both the nest and eggs agree closely with the other species of the genus to which the canary belongs." It is prolific with most other finches, and even with some which are usually considered as belonging to a different genus, such as the yellow hammer, *Emberiza citrinella*. The canary has been known to breed in confinement in this country six or eight times a year, and its age extends to fourteen or fifteen years.

2. *Varieties.*—Under the two great divisions al-

ready mentioned, the following long list of sub-varieties has been enumerated, which could be easily
extended, but to which it is of great importance
that the amateur should attend, as it will enable him
to judge more accurately of the value to be attached,
and the names to be ascribed, to the productions of
his breeding cage.—There are,

1. The common canary finch, of a grey colour,
with the down black ; as in the wild bird found in
the Canary Isles.

2. Grey canary finch, with the down and feet
white.

3. Grey canary finch, with white tail.

4. Common flaxen canary finch.

5. Flaxen canary finch, with red eyes.

6. Flaxen canary finch, with plumage glossed with
a golden hue.

7. Flaxen canary finch, with the down fair, or
unmixed with black.

8. Flaxen canary finch, with white tail.

9. Common yellow canary finch.

10. Yellow canary finch, with the down yellow,
and unmixed with black.

11. Yellow canary finch, with a white tail.

12. Common agate-coloured canary finch.

13. Agate-coloured canary finch, with red eyes.

14. Agate-coloured canary finch, with white tail.

15. Agate-coloured canary finch, with the down
of the same colour.

16. The common yellow dun-coloured canary
finch.

17. Yellow dun-coloured canary finch, with red
eyes.

18. Yellow dun-coloured canary finch, with plumage glossed with a golden hue.

19. Yellow dun-coloured canary finch, with the down of the same colour.

20. White canary finch, with red eyes.

21. Common variegated, or spangled canary finch.

22. Variegated canary finch, with red eyes.

23. Canary finch, variegated, with fair or flaxen colour.

24. Canary finch, variegated, with flaxen colour, and having red eyes.

25. Canary finch, variegated with black.

26. Canary finch, variegated with black and fine yellow, having red eyes.

27. Canary finch, regularly spangled with black and yellow.

28. Canary finch, entirely of a fine yellow.

29. Crested canary finches, some grey, yellow, and black crests.

The canary proves fertile and thrives best with the Serin and Citral. The Serin is a bird of small size, being not much larger than the common linnet. Its upper mandible is brown, the under whitish; the plumage above, brown, mixed with yellowish green; beneath, greenish yellow, and having the sides marked with spots of brown; the wings are marked with a greenish band; quills and tail brown, edged with greenish grey, and the legs brown. The Citral is larger than the Serin, has a louder note, and is found in Geneva, Switzerland, Italy, and Spain; the plumage above is of a yellowish green, spotted with brown; beneath a greenish yellow, wings dusky and greenish, and the legs flesh-colour.

These two have been frequently confounded with the common canary, it is therefore necessary to be thus particular in attending to their distinguishing characteristics, for although in reality essentially different in general appearance and habits, they are nearly assimilated.

The canary is not so tender nor so difficult to rear as is generally imagined. A good situation, however, is absolutely necessary. They cannot do without the warmth of the sun, but must be protected from the scorching glare of his beams. They should, therefore, always be placed near a window with a South-East, a South, or a South-Western exposure.

We tried to breed them in our own *sanctum* in the neighbourhood of Edinburgh, during the year 1837, but the window was a sky-light, sloping to the north —no direct sun-beam visited the cage—the birds were good and the hen laid well, but no egg was ever chipped. A villainous cat, a stranger too, tore her from her perch through the wires, without leaving a feather behind,—which prevented us from trying her in a better situation next year, where we have not the slightest doubt she would have completely succeeded. By cross-breeding and gradually accustoming the young to exposed situations, they will be brought to sing and thrive under almost any circumstances, but it must never be forgotten, that the warmth of the sun is indispensable for successful incubation. The original canary is in the estimation of the fancy now below par. Mules and the indefinite varieties produced by cross-breeding, are now (and justly) the favourites. Whatever they be, and by whatever name called, high authority has pronounced that they must possess the following characteristics—viz. a fine large cap or crown (extending over the whole of the back part of the head) of a deep rich orange colour, (not a lemon cast); and the same richness of ground must prevail in all its other parts, except where the rules prescribe black, viz. in the wings and tail, in which the feathers must be black home to the quill; the tail must have twelve black feathers, and each wing, eighteen feathers black to the quill. Their backs the first year are always more or less spangled or mottled; and the first time they change or moult their quill feathers they become lighter. Indeed, every season after the first, they change all their feathers lighter and lighter. Therefore, their beauty for prize showing is always in the first season, from seven to nine months old; and to produce a good breed, these requisites of feathers are as necessary in the hen as cock, which circumstance renders hens valuable.

Some object to the keeping of birds in cages altogether, and urge principle in favour of their prejudice, but this has been well stated in an excellent little book published by Mr. West of Glasgow, in the following terms: "The breeding and rearing of birds is so harmless and interesting an amusement, that the number of persons who indulge in it creates no surprise; indeed, the wonder would be were it otherwise. It is by no means said that persons who have a little spare time on their hands could not employ it to better purpose than the breeding of canaries; still, many persons employ such moments to purposes not half so pleasant, nor yet so innocently. For 'these splendid birds possess all those qualities that can soothe the heart or cheer the fancy; the brightest colours, the roundest forms, the most active manners, and the sweetest music.' And it is surely much better to breed canaries than guinea-pigs, or white mice!—the latter especially is very poor taste. Mice plague us enough sometimes, and we should not trouble ourselves to have them multiplied. Besides, it is not very consistent, in a land like ours, to wage a cruel and bloody war against the poor black, and to pet and pamper the whites.

" Talking of liberty, it has been said by some enthusiasts, that to confine birds in cages is cruel, and that no person who had truly the love of liberty at heart would be guilty of such an offence. But it is easy to see that this scruple cannot apply to canaries, or indeed to any completely domesticated bird; and instead of its being cruel to keep our canaries in cages, it would be much more so to turn them into the open air; for in meeting with liberty, they would also meet with death. It must have often been observed by persons in the habit of keeping domesticated birds, that they never show in any degree the least uneasiness on account of their confinement; but on the contrary, evince great fear when set at liberty, and are quite unhappy till they are safely lodged in their wiry tenement."

The canary is no lover of liberty; it has no desire to roam. Home, sweet home, is its favourite song, and it never appears to miss the tree in the land of its adoption. The cage is its palace—the perch is pleasanter to it than the carpeted parlour—there it loves and labours—it chaunts its note and builds its nest : and while many other prisoners pine in captivity, and sigh to be free, the canary, in its wiry cell, improves in feather and in song, and appears happier than its progenitors, when skimming the waters around their native isles. To produce, and to watch the production of some of the varieties of this beautiful bird, is at once an interesting study for the head, and a source of enjoyment to the heart, either of old or young. It forms great familiarity with man ; it shows even something like human vanity in being taken notice of, and something like human cunning in defeating the designs of those who would intercept its wilfulness ; we have had them to sit on the edge, and to drink out of our breakfast cup, but we never saw one that could be lured into the cage door till its own time came.

3. *Matching.*—Depth and richness of the orange-colour, is at present the prevailing taste in endeavouring to form a good match. In breeding fancy birds, a system so much practised in England, and on the Continent, and which is now rapidly extending over Scotland, the grand requisite is a regular and well feathered hen, on which every thing else depends. But the qualities of the cock to which she is to be united, ought not to be neglected. He, to have a good progeny, even with the best hen, ought to be bold, strong, and sprightly, with bright and sparkling eyes, erect carriage, symmetrical form, and sparrow-hawk-like posture on the perch. The most promis-

ing marks, however, may lead astray, if no inquiry is made, and no knowledge obtained of the family from which the pair have descended. Having obtained this information, and being certain that the stock is good, breeding may be safely attempted, and all turn out well, and far beyond expectation, even when all the points to be desired are not perceptible, for some of our most beautiful fancy varieties have arisen from accidental crossing, and when all the appearances were most unfavourable, and most unlikely, according to ordinary calculation, to lead to such a result. Much must depend upon the skill, judgment, knowledge, and taste, in the fanciers in canaries, as well as horses and dogs ; but as particular rules, when not too slavishly followed, under ignorance of the truth that the exception is the key-stone of the rule, are excellent auxiliaries to general principle, we subjoin seven, by attending to which, the amateur, with a little patience and practice, may produce varieties, not only to his own delight, but to the envy of others. He himself will soon be able to form many more for his own guidance, but for the present, we content ourselves with the number of perfection.

1. A fine, fancy, jonque cock, of a strong orange colour, with much black in his feathers, should be matched with a fine, soft coloured mealy hen, with as little black as possible, except her tail and wings, which must be regular and true.

2. For a strong mealy cock, a healthy jonque hen, with a fine soft feather, and regularly marked tail and wings, should be adopted ; and birds from the same

nest should never be joined, as this will reduce and weaken the progeny to a certainty.

3. Among the fancy breeding amateurs, strength of feather means a considerable quantity of black spangles on the back, and too much black colour in general when the belly feathers are blown asunder; and they are without silkiness or softness of feather, apparent in finer, richer coloured birds, which, when their belly feathers are breathed aside, feel fine, soft, and white, and they may be matched.

The fancy canary is of an orange colour, except the wings and tail, which are black; the cap or crown is of a very rich orange, extending over the whole back part of the head. Their backs, the first year, are always more or less mottled; and the first time they change or moult their quill feathers, they become lighter. Hence, their beauty for prize showing is always the first season, from seven to nine months old. Depth or richness of the orange colour is the grand object to be attended to in order to produce the real fancy; for the orange must not, by any means, be of the lemon cast. The male should be matched with a fine orange coloured mealy female, with the cap, wings, and tail regular, and with a fine feather.

4. For breeding with, mealy hens are always the most successful, because by their union with a spangle-marked cock, a more regular and finely marked cock is produced, than if the most beautifully spangled cock and hen had been the parents. According to St. Pierre, contrast is the law of nature. At all events, with regard to canaries this rule holds good,

that like should never be matched with like. Here extremes meet, and by the union excellent is the off-spring. Therefore, if one is weak, let it be matched with one that is strong ; if one is dark, let the other be fair; one spotted, let the other be plain ; if the one be crowned, let not even the shadow of a crown or coronet grace the brow of the other, and the excellence possessed by the one, which the other wants, will be found in higher perfection in the progeny than the single parent to which the happy quality belonged. In the feathered tribes, more than in all others, it will be found that the greatest harmony springs from opposition.

5. To produce a full coloured fine yellow bird, without spot or splash, which, next to fancy, is highly esteemed for its beauty, a fine large mealy hen, bred from a clean yellow stock, should be matched with a clean bred jonque cock. With every precaution, the most accurate attention, and the minutest observation, a spot or splash may appear in the brood, unless it is previously distinctly ascertained that the parent birds came from a clear bred stock. If any of the progenitors have been spotted or splashed, the defect may have leapt over one generation, and it may appear in the next.

6. Beautiful pie-coloured birds are produced by taking a fine clear jonque cock, matching him with a rich dark-coloured green or grey hen. By such a union the offspring will always be more or less pied ; they have in general an exceedingly clear pipe, and are reckoned not only strong, but sweet songsters.

7. That class of canaries whose feathers are be-

spangled all over with green and black, are called lizards, from the resemblance of their plumage to the coat of the reptile whose name they bear. By matching a pair of strikingly marked fancy birds, the strength of whose colours is glaring, that strong black mixture resembling the lizard is produced. The same result may also be obtained by matching a common strongly marked grey cock, with a splash-marked hen. Dark variegated birds may be got by a strong splashed common canary, with a fancy hen. Those that are all dark and sparrow-marked make fine singers. A strong grey or green canary, united to a mealy coloured hen, must be got to produce the cinnamon colour. Those of a lighter colour called quakers, that are sometimes produced, are not much esteemed. By following up for two or three seasons consecutively, mealies with mealies, white or flaxen coloured birds are produced, and by again crossing these with one with red eyes, another variety is obtained.

In the cottages of England, many of these varieties are reared with great care and judgment, but with little expense or trouble ; and are afterwards brought to Edinburgh and, Glasgow, where they bring high prices, and afford ample remuneration to the rearer. But why cause that to be imported to us, which could be so easily produced among ourselves? Could our children ever be more usefully or rationally employed, than in supplying the wants, studying the habits, and watching the peculiarities of tender creatures? Could a fair lady ever appear more interesting than when training her feathered favourite to hop from his wiry prison-house upon her lily finger, and in hear-

9

ing him pour forth from that lovely perch his melodious notes. All indeed seem to have a partiality for the canary, but few indulge the thought, and many assert the impossibility, of rearing him for themselves. But this we humbly apprehend is a grievous mistake, and we beg to hope, that by the multifarious modes of matching, which may be resorted to, when this interesting pursuit becomes more generally known, more splendid varieties than the world has yet seen will make their appearance, adding grace to the parlour and the drawing-room, gratifying the eye with the beauty of colour and form, and the ear with the melody of untaught music.

4. *Pairing.*—The proper period for putting the birds together for the purpose of pairing, depends very much on the nature of the weather. In general the month of March is the best time, although in some seasons it may be done a month earlier, and in others it is advisable to wait a month longer. Some people make a boast of their attempts at very early pairing, but it is a very idle boast, as precocious breeding is never profitable, both injuring the constitution of the parents, and turning out in general an inferior brood. Young birds have been produced even before this period, but it is at a great sacrifice, and under disadvantages which will tell before the end of the season. They must be brought up, and at the early period of their existence, must subsist without that green food with which at a later period their parents, and afterwards themselves, could be so abundantly supplied. What is gained in time is lost in power, as

in the summer months there will be less inclination and less capacity for incubation.

Common canaries that have spent the winter together, may indeed be put into the breeding cage and left to themselves ; in these circumstances they seldom breed too early, but it is also true they seldom breed well. It is better to separate them for a short time. Their long familiarity is apt to induce indifference, the greatest enemy to love, but after a short separation, old acquaintance is soon renewed, old love is speedily kindled, and you may calculate almost to an hour when the hen will begin to lay.

Some breeders put the birds intended for breeding into a small cage, with only one upper perch, to make them familiar and sociable with each other. Others put them at first into the cage appointed for breeding ; the former method is allowed to be the best for fancy breeding.

During the time they are pairing, they should be fed high, by giving them sparingly every morning a little chopped egg and bread, mixed with a little maw seed, and some bruised hemp seed. As soon as they become sociable, feed each other, and sleep on the perch close together, then the breeding cage for their reception may be prepared.

It is needful to remark, some birds at first pairing will fight very much, and the hen strive for the mastership, but in most cases, to the courage of the male be it spoken, without success. If they should fight too much, and will not come to any reconciliation in the course of one month's trial, it will be best to part them and try another hen.

These birds have their sympathies and antipathies, which nothing can subdue. The sympathy of a male has been shown by putting him alone in an aviary, where there are many females ; in a few hours he will make choice of one, and will not cease for an instant to show his attachment, by feeding her. Nay, he will even choose a female without seeing her ; it is sufficient that he should hear her cry, and he will not cease to call her. The same observation is also applicable to the female, and her being already bespoke has been known to prove fatal ; when the new lover has died of grief.

In some cases however all these sources of sympathy seem to be dried up within them, and an immediate antipathy, which no endearment nor fond caress can overcome, to have usurped its place. By no contrivance can such canaries be brought to pair. More cocks than hens appear thus constituted, and these cocks are generally found to be the best singers.

Though sufficiently fond, they are not so faithful, as Addison in his pretty lines in the Spectator appears to imagine—

> " Chaste are their instincts, faithful is their fire ;
> No foreign duty tempts to false desire."

This may be consistent enough with the fancy of the poet, but not with the practice of the fancier. They are by no means strictly monogamous. The cock, indeed, never aspires to the harem of the Sultan, but he might often be indicted for bigamy were a sentence even of perpetual imprisonment to him any punishment.—Either cock or hen will, in general circumstances, very readily take up with another mate. It is also evident that their attachment is not confined to those of their own kind, as the beautiful variety of mules which has sprung from the canary and other tribes of finches abundantly testifies.

The birds having at length been successfully paired, all now depends upon season, situation, and cage.

With regard to the season, we have already said it is better to be too early than too late. If March has been cold, and no favourable change takes place in April, they should be kept back as long as possible, as in such a season the hen is apt to become egg-bound, or to lay soft eggs : in the one case her life is endangered—in the other, her strength is wasted in vain.

The situation is a matter of very considerable importance. To this we have already alluded, but must repeat more particularly that it should if possible be exposed to the sloping beams of the morning sun, and protected from his meridian rays. If the sun does not leave the situation before noon, it is easy to cast the cage into shadow by a screen at a distance from it.—Pulling down the window-blinds, or placing chicken-weed on the top of the cage, to overhang the sides in festoons, is a simple process. When the weather is close and sultry, the window may be opened early, and when hot, left open all day ; but *cuvete lupis*—take care of cats. For many reasons the doors should be shut, draughts of air being as pernicious to the eggs as feline intruders are to the birds. As the best situation to gain the morning sun and escape the north-easterly gales is S. by E., S.S.E., S.E. by S., or S.E., and not direct east, it is frequently cool from these points even in the month of May—precautions must be taken accordingly; but an excess of heat is as prejudicial as cold. Too much warmth and want of air is apt to give the hen the sweating sickness while sitting, and to render the young weak and tender.

The room into which the pair are placed should never require a fire; hence an additional reason for not beginning too early; it should neither be damp, dark, nor close, but dry, large, light, and airy. A cheerful situation and the morning sun give spirit, warmth, and animation to the birds. If draughts of air can be prevented and cats excluded during summer, the window should be thrown completely open all day. If a good wire gauze can be made to project from the window, the birds can easily be placed under it, where they will get the air and enjoy the warmth without the scorching heat of the sun.

The place for the birds to breed in having been chosen, the next consideration is the best kind of cage to hang up for their reception. If an old one is adopted, it ought to be thoroughly washed, scrubbed, rubbed, cleaned, and dried. After their long cessation from use, vermin of various sorts are apt to lodge in the crevices, which, if not utterly exterminated, will grieve the heart both of bird and breeder. The cage should be so placed as to admit of a constant

view of the birds and an easy access without disturb-
ing them. They should not be hung, unless for dis-
agreeable reasons, and in disadvantageous circumstances, out of reach, requiring to be lifted or drawn
down to us, or to take stools or steps to get to them.
They should at least be on a level with the line of
vision. This familiarizes the birds with their keeper,
makes him better acquainted with them, he can see
at a glance what is going on, they become accustomed to any little motion or commotion that may be
going on around, they will be less liable to be frightened and flustered by the appearance of danger, and
in every respect the breeding cage will become a
more manageable commodity than it generally is.

Of the structure of the cage we shall afterwards
take notice, but the one for breeding should have two
nest boxes at one end, that the birds may have choice,
always having the perches clean, and as stout as their
claws can grasp and stand firm upon, likewise clean
claws, without lumps of dirt on them; for by having
a steady, full sized perch, the birds hold fast, and
when they tread they have no trouble or the fear of
falling or slipping, or turning round on the perch,
which is against a sure *tread,* and produces addled
eggs.

Some breeders pair a strong healthy male with
two females, which in some cases does pretty well,
provided that proper attention is paid to them. When
two hens are intended to be put up with one male,
they should be selected for that purpose at the end
of harvest, and kept in one cage during the winter,

in order to make them familiar with each other. It will not do to put two hens with a male in one cage without there being a temporary board in the middle, to prevent the hens from seeing each other while they are hatching, or they will fly off their nests at each other, and fight like two little termagants, and in the scuffle the eggs, and consequently the hopes of the breeder, may be upset. But to prevent such vexations, let the breeder have two cages, and put up only one hen at a time, and after she has done laying, take the male out and put him up with the other hen, and so on to the end of the season.

Sprinkle plenty of gravel or sea-sand at the bottom of your cage, and hang up in it a lump of good old mortar, the nibbling and biting of which keeps the birds in good health. As soon as you have put your birds up, keep feeding them high, and add a little moist sugar to the bread and egg until they have laid an egg or two ; the moist sugar opening the hens' bodies, and preventing them being egg-bound. Be sure the bread and egg are fresh every day ; and it is best to feed them over-night, so that they find it early and fresh at break of day. Let the greens be always fresh, such as water cresses, radish tops, cos lettuce, cabbage lettuce, small sallad, as cresses, mustard, &c., all young and green. I do not recommend chickweed, nor groundsel ; nor plantain till it is ripe and full of seed.

5. *Breeding.*—The Canary is a most prolific bird, so much so, that in the great majority of instances the propensity requires to be restrained rather than encouraged. They will have from two to five nests

in the year ; and a few years ago a celebrated fancier in Stirlingshire, had a canary which brought up safely and successfully eight broods in one season. But this was an experiment which he thought it cruel to make, and which it would be imprudent to repeat. They should not be allowed to breed more than twice, or at the most three times a year. If a hen is prolific one season, she will be the reverse the next, or she may be completely destroyed by the effort. One that has two or three nests, and four or five eggs each time, must be a mother sufficiently valuable, and to overtax her is both unwise and unsafe.

The period of incubation lasts fourteen days, but in very warm weather, the process may be completed in thirteen days. Between seven and nine in the morning is their regular time of laying, and for the purpose of preventing waste of time, by permitting the hen to sit on unfecundated eggs, some breeders are in the habit of taking the eggs out when about eight days old, and holding them between their finger and thumb before a strong light, when it is ascertained that those which are transparent are unimpregnated and therefore useless, but the good ones are dark and thick. If they are all bad they should be thrown away; the nest should be taken out, shaken and cleaned, and an inducement and an opportunity afforded the hen to lay again, which she will generally do in a very short time. After laying two or three eggs some hens will desert them, and it is found upon examination, that these eggs are in general bad ; nature, by some mysterious process, giving the bird an instinctive hint, that to brood over them longer, would be love's labour lost. These, therefore, should be immediately broken, and the hen allowed to go to nest again. We confess it seems strange, that when nature tells the little creature so much, it does not teach her to do this for herself; for this however there may be many wise reasons, as it would be teaching her a very bad habit, which is one of the worst of things, either in feathered or unfeathered bipeds.

It is recommended by some breeders, as soon as the canary has laid, to take out the egg every morning and substitute an ivory one; when the hen has done laying, take the ivory eggs away, and set her upon the whole of her own. Naturalists say that it gives the hen more satisfaction to see them come successively one after the other; but experience has shown us that it is the better way to substitute the ivory egg, and daily take away the laid one, till she lays her complement; and also to examine the eggs after the hen has been sitting eight days upon them, to save time and useless fatigue to the mother; let all this, however, be done with as little annoyance as possible.

Some females in breeding are very careless mothers, a fault which is not easily done away with. Therefore, if they cannot be brought to do any thrift the first season, avoid another season's trial. Others will eat their eggs, as will sometimes also the male. The best way to prevent this, is to feed the bird very early every morning with bread and egg, or the last thing at night for the morning, for the hen no sooner

lays her egg than she leaves the nest and flies round
the cage in search of food, which if she does not find,
and that too in some delicate and dainty form, she returns to the nest in a rage and seems to break the
eggs out of pure spite, more than from a desire to eat
them. As another precaution when the hen is addicted to this vice, the usual period for the laying of
canaries should be carefully watched, and as soon as
she has left it, the egg she has laid should be removed and the ivory ball substituted, and if this is
done for four or five mornings, all the eggs may be
returned, when there is a great chance of her settling
down and sitting the requisite time. When the male
eats the eggs, it is a sign of strength, through good
feeding. Such males should have two hens.

It will frequently happen with young mothers,
that the first time of hatching they are so careful
and anxious for the eggs that are not hatched, as not
to leave their nest to feed the young that are hatched,
and the consequence is, that the young birds are
starved. The best preventive of this evil is to attend to the day they will be hatched, by keeping a
register of the time when they were laid and set.
The most enticing food, such as bread and egg, fresh
greens, &c., should be placed before them, to remind
them of the duty of feeding their young. If the hen
is not observed feeding her young, or carrying
food to them, she should be stirred out of the nest, to
let her see that there is enough to satisfy her wants.
If this is done three or four times the first day, by
feeding as she goes out, and seeing her young ones
gape as she comes in, she will soon be brought to feed

them, and the cock will soon follow her example. With every care to set the hen exactly to a day, it will happen that all the eggs are not chipped at the same time ; when this contingence takes place, every effort must be made to allure them to their duty, as we can scarcely conceive it within the range of mere instinct to inform them that there is ever laid upon them a double obligation. If there is any suspicion that either nest or eggs are damaged, the hen may be driven off to ascertain the fact. On this account it is of importance that the eggs should be so placed that you may come at the birds with ease to observe their actions, without annoying them.

The technical terms and names given to young birds in general are a *Nestling*, or one from the nest ; a *Pusher*, a young bird that is taken three or four days after he has left his nest ; a *Brancher* is a bird full grown, but has his nestling feathers. This last is the best state to take linnets, goldfinches, chaffinches, and hedge sparrows. It is not advantageous to take them in their first partial moult, as the change of diet and confinement frequently produces ill health, by spoiling the moult. The hedge sparrows, though much despised, if taken when branchers and brought up for singing, will take the canary song so well, that you would not know them apart ; and the linnet brought up at this period may be taught any song, and become noted for that of the wood lark. The brancher chaffinch may be broken into any song so perfectly, that many would scarcely believe him to be a chaffinch. The goldfinch does not come up to the linnet, chaffinch, or hedge sparrow for singing, but excels in plumage and producing fine coloured pied mules.

Some breeders bring up young canaries by hand, which is very troublesome ; for you must feed them very early in the morning, and every two hours during the day, but it must be done in precisely the same way and with the same food as with linnets. As they are almost the only birds which we take delight in pairing for breeding, the satisfaction we have in supplying them with necessaries both for food and building, in observing their little courtships when pairing, their dexterity in building their nest, the readiness of the male to take his turn in all the duties of building, hatching and feeding, together with the continual melody wherewith they charm us,—all afford a pleasure as serene and exquisite as any we can feel. In my humble opinion, such little offices are preferable to any we can perform for them. If a cock or hen should die, early in the breeding season, and it is worth while, having time in hand, you must choose a mate as near as possible in colour, age, and size to the deceased ; for there is always most sympathy with those that resemble their own choice.

As for cleanliness, air, and exercise, when birds have brought up a nest of young ones, watch the opportunity to clean out the nest box, and if this be very dirty, throw away the dirt and nest. Then let the birds have plenty of clean materials, and you will soon see them build another nest ; and I have frequently known them to build another nest in one day. Neglect of the main point, cleanliness, which promotes health, and keeps away the red mites. causes many breeders much trouble, vexation, and disappointment.

When the breeding season is over, and the birds all put into the cages, let them not be fed with much green food ; indeed, at no time give much, as it is better to give none at all, than too much. Beginners cannot be cautioned enough regarding this, as many hundreds of canaries die every year from no other cause than being surfeited with green meat.

6. *Mule Breeding.*—Some naturalists are of opinion that the hybrid of the canary forms an exception, and instead of being barren is fruitful, and can propagate its kind. Baron Cuvier, in his "Animal Kingdom," states this doctrine, but only to disprove it. The same opinion was taken up by Goldsmith, who only derived it from books, and is also maintained by several eminent naturalists. The same is said, if we remember rightly, of the progeny of the partridge and pheasant, but in both cases equally without foundation. *A priori*, we might pronounce it contrary to an established law of nature, as all observation attests it to be notoriously contrary to the fact. From experience, tried by many individuals, sometimes with great patience for a long series of years, no fertility has ever been found to follow. Eggs will be laid and all the duties of mothers performed, but here the matter ends ; and this no more implies the reproductive power of the canary mule, than the laying and setting of the domestic fowl without a cock. But although no posterity follows, the first operation

is sufficiently interesting to make the subject of mule breeding worthy of attention.

There are various kinds of cross breeding, or what is termed mule breeding ; that is, a union with other country finches, or small hard billed birds, such as the Venturon, the Cini or Serin, the Aberdevine, the English Goldfinch, Greenfinch, Chaffinch, Linnet, Hedge Sparrow, Yellow Hammer, and Bullfinch, united with the cock and hen canaries ; which require some notice and attention.

None in this country is so common as the union of the goldfinch and linnet ; therefore, the following observations and experience may be of use. Goldfinches should be completely domesticated. It is best to have them quite young, on purpose to train them up well to eat the rape and canary seeds, which improve their feather, color, and health. Gross hemp seed ultimately rots them, and changes the brightness and colour of their plumage to brown.

To breed with the cock goldfinch and hen canary, if not trained, and there is no respect paid to age, get a strong healthy cock, caught in the beginning of the month of April, for then he is considered rank, seeking his mate :

> " All nature seems at work : slugs leave their lair—
> The bees are stirring—birds are on the wing—
> And Winter, slumbering in the open air,
> Wears on his smiling face a dream of Spring."
> COLERIDGE.

If he can be prevented from being sulky on account of his confinement and change of diet, he may make a good husband. But if the change should produce scouring, which it is very apt to do, he must be fed for a time on hemp and flax seed, with some scraped chalk given him into his cage. Thistle-seed, especially that of the great white thistle, which is his favourite, will tend greatly to counteract and cure the complaint. He may then be paired with a canary, and if the young ones are marked with tolerably equal portions of colour, they may be considered handsome birds.

The general way is to pair the hen canary with the cock goldfinch or cock linnet; but it is far better to pair the cock canary with the hen goldfinch and hen linnet. It is, however, far harder to domesticate and break the latter in than a canary hen, for which reason they are seldom tried. The breed from the cock canary is stronger and finer, and inherits more of the canary song. The breed from a cock linnet and hen canary are never equal in beauty of feather to the breed of the cock goldfinch and hen canary; but in song they are the best of all the mule productions. The young from a cock canary and hen goldfinch differ very much in beauty; some have turned out quite white, although this is rare and valuable on account of its variety. This case may occur if the cock was beautiful, clear, mealy, strong, and in good health. Those of a bluish cast generally spring from a greenfinch cock and hen canary: those of the bullfinch are scarce, but are susceptible of a good education, and their plumage is singular, but their alliance rarely thrives.

It appears from experience, that of all birds coupled with the canary, the serin finch has the strongest voice, and is the most vigorous and ardent for propagation. It also appears, that it is the only one whose mules are fertile, which argues close affinity if not identity of species.

There is likewise great sympathy between the siskin and canary; and the former will, in a state of nature, seek the society of canaries. Mr. Willoughby calls the Aberdevine the siskin, from its name, Seisel, by which this bird is known in Austria and the south of France. It is a merry little bird, and arrives in England every spring. It is known in Sussex by the name of the harley bird, being always found there at the above season of the year. Its plumage is of a yellow green cast; it resembles the canary in feather, but is smaller, and the song is soft and pleasing, and when in health it is a merry, lively bird. The Germans, it is said, are fond of pairing the siskin with the canary. Those who have tried in England have found no advantage arising from it, as they produce a small breed, and no improvement in voice or feather.

Much experience, attention to nature, and observation, are required in cross or mule-breeding, to domesticate and break in the birds to the canary food, and to know their age. For example: linnets should not be turned up to breed till two years old, when crossed with the canary. A goldfinch hen ought to be two years old, as she seldom lays eggs the first year in a cage. And, observe nature in putting your birds up to breed: that is, to fall in about their own natural time, be the bird whatever it may. You must not expect mule or cross breeding to be ever

10

prolific ; the Aberdevine and Serin finches are the most prolific, (probably this is the reason the Germans choose them to breed from,) the goldfinch next, and the linnet seldom more than one nest in a season.

To domesticate and rear up young goldfinches, linnets, chaffinches, hedge sparrows, bullfinches, &c., it would not be amiss to get their eggs from the nest, and set them under the canary hen, in the same manner that many fancy breeders keep a good gay breeding hen to hatch and breed up the fancy canaries' eggs.

In the finch tribe, it may be noticed there are two distinct and separate species ; the one hard-billed, living upon seed ; the other soft-billed, living on flesh, soft food, and insects. Any of the hard-billed birds may be paired with the canary, the others will not unite. Mule breeding will do best in the country, as good air and a lively situation is essential for breeding with any thing like success. Those who wish to amuse themselves with mule-breeding, must not feel disappointed in losing for a season or two. It is always with the greatest difficulty that any thing is produced from the greenfinch, bullfinch, chaffinch, or yellow-hammer. Therefore, it is better to take the eggs of these finches, and let them be hatched and brought up by canary mothers.

As mules will not breed, some do not like such a race of hens thrown upon their hands useless, but it is affirmed that there are more males by far than females. If this be true, there is some little recompense in mule breeding.

This is the whole that is deemed necessary to advance on this subject. A great deal more might have been said, but as it will require a little experience to become acquainted with the general method of mule-breeding, which cannot be got by any thing we could say, we therefore leave that part to the reader, confident that a little attention and observation will overcome any difficulties to which he may be exposed.

7. *Feeding.*—The seed that now universally goes by its own name is the common food of the canary, and on it alone it thrives sufficiently, especially when kept single as the "pet of the parlour," and merely for the purposes of song ; but when intended for breeding and to produce fancy varieties, something more is required. High feeding is essential to them from the first moment they are set to pair till the time they are separated, and this is generally composed of animal food and hard boiled egg mixed with seed. The egg should always be fresh, and if possible newly laid. The egg, when boiled hard, should be chopped, and mixed with dry stale grated bread or roll, in quantity proportionally greater than that of the egg itself. A little soft sugar, with some mawseed, is an excellent addition, and with these they will rear up their young healthy and well. It is recommended to place a small cup in the cage containing a few groats, which form a very substantial diet, to which a zest will be given by a supply of some green food, such as chick-weed, groundsel, or ripening dandelion tops, gathered—let it ever be remembered—fresh every morning. All stale food and refuse of every kind should be daily removed, and if this is not attended to, gripes and hoarseness

in the young birds will be the consequence—evils
more easily prevented than removed.   Night is better than morning for supplying the more substantial
food, as at the first peep of dawn they will find their
repast fresh, clean, and tidy, of which they will partake with a keener relish than after their appetite
has been clogged with garbage.   In the morning,
greens, water cresses, radish tops, cabbage lettuce,
should be given, fresh and sparingly ; and if chickweed or groundsel is given, let them be ripe, and not
much at a time.   Some persons keep their birds entirely on rape seed ; but it is too relaxing, and ultimately kills them.   Canaries should always be allowed plenty of clean water and gravelly soil.   Besides
water for drinking, they should be allowed twice a
week some to wash themselves ; a saucer is the best
vessel for holding it.   The female, while hatching,
should not get water to wash herself, as that might
retard the incubation, and even run a chance of rot-
ting the eggs.

8. *Cages.*—The forms of cages deemed suitable for
finches, are as various as the fancies of the purchaser, or the tastes of the wire-workers.   Some con-
tend for them being small, while others cannot have
them large enough, the former only regarding the
singing—the latter, air and exercise.   For their respective objects, each has its advantages.   The mere
shape is altogether a matter of taste, for it does not
signify much, unless for breeding, when an oblong is
evidently the only proper form.   For this purpose,
the kind now most in use, are about 18 inches by 11,
and 12 in height ; the perches are placed four inch-

es and a half from the ends of the cage, to keep the tails clear, which will allow 7 inches of a leap, which is long enough. The nest box is placed on the outside, at the end of the cage, and is not a fixture, but can be removed at any time. Those cages with two perches below, and one above, in the middle of the two below, should not be used, as they tend to diminish the stately appearance of the birds; but those with only two perches on a level, give birds by far the best shape. The cage should be thickly and firmly wired, to prevent, as much as possible, the mischief frequently done by mice, who often eat the eggs, and even the young ones. If the birds are attacked by a cat, which also happens, they have the best chance of escaping that are in a closely wired cage, provided it be firmly fixed up. The wire should always be of iron, as canaries are ever nibbling at it; brass wires become wet, and get covered with poisonous verdigris, which is not good for birds. It is recommended to have cages painted, either inside or out, with common oil paint; they may be varnished on the outside, or colored with lime wash, mixed with a little blue or green, as the reflection of white weakens the sight. All cages should have a large door in front of them, which is very convenient for many purposes.

In purchasing an old cage, or putting up breeding cages which may have been out of use for some time, see that they are not beset with red mites, like bugs in old furniture; and that there are no old looking, dry, musty places about the hinges, doors, or nest boxes. Wash them well with strong yellow soap-

suds and pearl ashes ; and when dry, they may be
washed over with the following lotion : spirit of tur-
pentine, and spirit of wine, equal parts ; in which
dissolve some camphor and soda, about the size of a
scarlet bean ; mix this well together, and keep it in
a bottle, closely corked, for use ; before using it,
shake it up, and dip into it a small brush, with which
wash over the cage, and let it dry for a day or two
in any airy place to carry off the smell.   This de-
stroys all the red mites and other vermin that lurk in
the crevices, and that in the heat of summer would
pour forth their hosts to annoy the birds both old
and young.   Soak the water glasses and fountains
in pearl-ash and water for a few minutes, to cleanse
them from scurf and green.   Here it may be thought
proper to notice what is termed the stock cage, so
much in use by the fancy breeders in England.   This
cage is about one foot in width, nine inches in height,
and nine inches in depth, with a wire front only, and
a groove to run a glass in, to shut them close, or admit air, at pleasure ; the top of the cage is half wired,
and made with a flat leaf, to cover or open as may
be thought necessary, and through which to view the
inmates.   Immediately after the young birds leave
their parents, they are put into one of these cages,
where they are kept warm, which throws them into
an artificial fever, and this produces the moult.   The
first moult is only partial, as only their nest feathers
fall off, when they are in full plumage.

It is thought that heat and closeness produce a
fine soft feather, and the finer the feather, the brighter will be the colour.   But it must not be concealed,

that scarcely one out of three survives this operation.
Seldom more than one bird is put into such a cage,
for fear they should fight and pluck each other's
feathers.

Stock cages are very convenient to have at hand,
for sick birds, to nurse and bring them about ; but we
do not approve of the use that is generally made of
them. No doubt, in time of moulting, it is necessary to be careful of birds ; and, should their moult
seem to proceed slowly, cover the cage round with
paper, leaving the front open, putting a little saffron
in their water, to assist them to throw off their feathers, as they have not the exercise they would have
in a state of nature. But to keep birds so closely as
is done in these cages makes them weak and delicate,
analogous to green-house plants, and incapable of
standing the least cold ; so much so, that some have
died when caught, with the fluttering and cold touch
of the hand. Even at the best of times, when moult-
ed from one of these cages, they must be considered
as green-house plants, and dealt with accordingly.
But by pursuing the ordinary method, great trouble
is saved, and fine healthy, lively, and strong birds
reared, capable of standing most situations.

9. *Building.*—The materials used and recommended for building are numerous and varied, but the
principal points to be attended to are warmth and
cleanliness. Of whatever stuff the nest is composed
it should always be new. The materials of the old
nest must be unscrupulously rejected, unless it is
wished to colonize the new one with red mites, and
all sorts of vermin. All old fabrics indeed are bad,

as from them the woolly surface has been much rubbed off, and little but the cold fibre left behind.

The wooden cup, box, or basket, should have put
into it a little fine fresh clean elk's hair mixed with
soft dried moss, and some white wool neatly disposed, so as to give as little trouble as possible to the
bird in forming it into the shape of a nest. Previous
to doing so, we ourselves have often successfully,
although we know not whether it has been sanction-
ed or practised by others—rubbed the inside of the
nest box with strong warm glue, and while in a liquid state allowed it to retain as much wool as could
be gently dipped upon it, while the roll was instantly
lifted up. This forms a fixed and warm foundation.
We have also lined our boxes with undressed fur, and
have found that although the materials afterwards
placed upon it were scanty, the nest was sufficiently
warm for successful incubation.

About a handful of these should be put into the
nest and hung up in the cage, which, with the pre-
paration previously made in the breeding apartment,
the birds will find little trouble in forming their nests.

Sometimes before the young are ready to quit one
nest, the hen will feel a desire to build another. This
she will sometimes do, even on the top of her young,
and thus smother them.

10. *Sex.*—It is not at all times easy to distinguish
between cock and hen. By an experienced fancier,
it can be done indeed at a glance, and some are even
able to point out the cocks almost as soon as they
are hatched.

Both the size and the singing are pretty good dis-

tinguishing marks between male and female, but sometimes even these are not sufficient, as many a gigan-
tic hen has been found, and as there have been crow-
ing hens in the barn yard, they have not been altogether banished from the canary cage. Some females, by their musical attempts, have deceived the
unskilful, and sometimes even the knowing ones
have been taken in, and have remained sceptical till
the reputed gentleman began to lay eggs. This is
the most conclusive test of all. A hen may try to
sing, but no cock, us far as we know, has ever attempted to lay eggs. But the sure way to distinguish
the female's jabbering from the legitimate song of the
male is, that though a male may sing ever so indif-
ferently, every time he strikes a note, the passage of
his throat will heave with a pulsive motion, and continue so all the time he is singing; but let the female sing ever so well, this motion is never observed
in her throat as in the male's. Another way to distinguish the male from the female is, the color above
the bill, under the throat, and the pinion of the wings,
is of a brighter hue in the male; for let birds be of
what shade of color they may, the male will always
have a brighter yellow on the above-mentioned
places, which is always pale and languid in the female. But what is as good a criterion as any other,
is the largeness, vigor, and majestic carriage of the
male, which he always shows, if in good health, by
stretching himself out to his utmost extent. The female is generally smaller and shorter, especially from
the legs to the vent, and of a more sudden roundness,
required by nature for containing and laying her

eggs; the male in that part is slim and long, ending
in a small point under the tail.

11. *Singing.*—According to Lucretius, the song of
birds is the source of all music. What from them it
was first our privilege to derive, it is now our pleasure to communicate, that it may be received back
again in delightful reciprocity. The origin of music
in every country has been from the woods and lawns.
The most ancient melodies, in their simple pathos
and plaintive wildness, give evident proof that the
songsters of the grove first formed the taste and
tuned the ear of the earliest musicians. The shepherd's reed or pipe, of few notes, and of the plain *dia-
tonic scale*, without semi-tones, flats, or sharps, was
plainly first formed to imitate the song of birds. All
the music that science has formed, or art has taught,
is founded upon the sounds that Nature furnishes.

Et zephiri cava per calamorum sibila primum,
Agrestais docuere cavas inflare cicutas.

In this point of view, even the canary assumes
somewhat of a dignified attitude, and for it high ho-
nor might be claimed, as from the facility of its domestication it can be made to bring so much of the
music of the groves to our hearts and to our homes.

Even those who have no soul for artificial music,
and who remain unmoved under the energetic strains
of a Braham, and unmelted by the sweet warblings
of a Stephens, have listened with delight to the carol
of the lark, or the note of the nightingale. No poetry
has ever warmed the heart of him whose ear has not
been charmed with music. No one can touch the
golden lyre whose heart-strings have not vibrated at

the native wood-note wild. Poetry and music are
two sisters ever inseparably entwined in one fond
embrace. The voice may indeed be unable to modu-
late the melody with which the ear is filled, the lips
may be unable to extract its sound from the flute,
the fingers may grate across the strings of the violin
—in every musical instrument we may lose our cunning, but we have a never-failing friend to supply the
place of them all.

De gustibus non disputandum, therefore, no certain
rules can be laid down with regard to the singing of
the canary, by which all will be satisfactorily guid-
ed. All birds, indeed, are agreeable in their different
songs; the sky-lark, for his vast compass of natural
notes; the linnet, for his docility in imitating regular
music, and taking the wood-lark's song; and the goldfinch, for his agreeableness and attachment to his
house.

Canaries, with long, straight and tapering bodies,
are found, by observation, to be the finest in song,
while, on the contrary, short, thick-set cocks are
found to be harsh and abrupt in their notes, and to be
deficient in the power of their lungs. When it is desired to make young canaries good songsters, they
should, if possible, be put under the nightingale or
tit-lark for tuition. The German method, but we
beg to doubt its propriety, to produce fine songsters,
is to cover the cage all day and to expose the birds
in the evening to a strong light, when by making any
noise, they are induced to sing. It is better to place
two or three birds together, as they will vie with
each other.

12. *Teaching.*—The canary bird, when young, can be taught almost any tune by means of whistling, the flageolet, or bird-organ. It is best to teach them by recording their own notes as soon as they are able to feed themselves. Whatever may be the instrument used to teach them, it should be sweet and mellow in its tone. For further instructions, better cannot be given than those of the celebrated Lewis De Berg, which he gives in the following remarks :

"There is neither lark, linnet, bullfinch, nor goldfinch," says this celebrated bird-fancier, "but that may be brought to as great perfection in song as the canary finch, but the English do not take the pains a German does; they love to sleep, while the German is tuning his pipe and instructing his feathered songster. There is more to be done with the lark from two or three o'clock in the morning, than can be done in many months in the day-time, or when the least noise or sound is to be heard but from the instructor ; and this rule holds good with all finches. Every thing should be quiet but the master. As it is with the human kind, so it is with the feathered : a good master often makes a good scholar ; and a good tutor seldom fails of making a good bird. I say, begin with your birds when all is quiet ; they will then take much more notice of what you endeavor to teach them. The age for beginning to instruct should not exceed three months. I sometimes begin sooner, and seldom stay less than an hour with each bird. I sometimes use my pipe, sometimes whistle, sometimes sing, but whichever method I adopt, seldom fail of bringing up birds to please ; insomuch, that I have

often sold a lark for two guineas; a linnet for one
guinea; a bullfinch, when it could pipe finely, from
five to ten guineas; and a goldfinch from one to two
guineas. In short, the whole of bringing up a bird
to sing well, depends entirely on visiting him early,
and furnishing him the last thing before you leave
him, with what he is to eat for the day. He should
be supplied daily with fresh water in his fountain,
and small gravel at the bottom of his cage; but short
allowance in eating is absolutely necessary to make
him a good songster. When I come to him in the
morning, he is glad to see me; supposing him hungry, (says the German) he will soon begin to talk to
me, and bid me welcome. At first approaching my
bird, I very often give him three or four grains of
rice, which have been steeped in canary. I sometimes add a little saffron or cochineal to the water,
according as I find my bird in health and strength,
and I seldom fail of being rewarded with a song for
my pains. In the general way of feeding the larks,
I give a small quantity of bruised rice, with egg and
bread, and now and then a few hemp seeds. I feed
the smaller birds with rape seed, and a very little
canary with it, the latter being apt to make them
grow fat and dull. I give them likewise at times a
little bruised rice, which does abundance of service,
and most assuredly prevents their falling into a scouring, which is the death of many a fine bird. Birds
accustomed to this way of feeding are seldom trou-
bled with what is called the pip; they shed their
feathers with far more ease than other birds, are in
general much prone to singing, and have a more

agreeable note than birds that have not been so trained.

"The reader should observe that when I order grains of bruised rice to be given, I always expect that the rice had been first soaked in canary wine, and afterwards dried carefully for use, (though giving a bird occasionally a few grains whilst they are wet or moist, with this excellent liquor, does mighty well, but it is not to be constantly practised;) the rice is only to be roughly bruised, so as to make it tender, and consequently easier to be eaten by the birds. I have observed many people in England give birds loaf sugar, which is a great error. I advise in its place a small lump of bay salt or cuttle-bone, and now and then a drop or two of the spirits of nitre in their water. If you proceed according to these directions, you will find your birds equal to those of any other nation."

13. *Diseases.*—If proper care is taken, the canary is subject to few diseases. Those that do arise, may all be traced to carelessness and inattention. If duly fed, their cages regularly cleaned and kept in good air, it is seldom that the birds are found in bad health. In a state of nature they are liable to many misfortunes, but what are their diseases the records of no ornithological hospital can tell. In a state of domestication their health can be better observed and more carefully attended to, and some hints can be given how it may be preserved or restored.

Colds are the most general complaint, and they are almost all owing to carelessness. How frequently are birds hung up close to the top corner of a win-

dow, with the sash down about one foot, and a draught
of air running through or by the cage fit to turn a
windmill. Thus they are frequently exposed for several hours late in the evening, when going to roost,
without any consideration whether the air be damp,
cold, or dry. In this manner many a fine bird is endangered, if not killed, by taking cold, which often
proves incurable.

When birds are in good health, and lively, their
feathers will appear and feel sleek and smooth, ad-
hering close to their bodies. Whenever you perceive
the reverse of this, and the birds are sitting dull and
bunchy, rely on it something is out of order. Therefore, first consider the season or time of year ; if
moulting is approaching, or if any thing has worried
or frightened the bird ; if he has been hung up in a
draught of air and taken cold ; if he is suffering from
neither of these causes, see if he can get at his water
and seed, and that both are sweet ; good seed always
appears clear and glossy, and feels dry and hard ; if
there is no fault here, examine his body, blow up the
feathers of his belly, see if his bowels look swelled or
inflamed, and if so, it is symptomatic of a surfeit.
If he appears lean and out of condition, look narrow-
ly for vermin about his body, and examine well his
cage for those small red mites which assail him at
night when gone to roost, and frequently are the cause
of his picking and plucking himself so much by day.
Likewise, such is the susceptibility of the canary
finch through delicate breeding, above all other
finches, that frequently you will cause him to begin
to moult, if the place or room should be close or

warm, compared with what he has been accustomed
to ; and a change from a warm room to a cold one
will make him bunchy and dull, and stop his singing.
In purchasing a bird, careful inquiry should be made
as to the quarter from which he came, and the temperature to which he was accustomed. If a stock
cage has been used, the greatest caution is necessary
in removing the bird to an open one. It need not
surprise any one if he should appear dull and sulky
when removed from light and cheerful company, to a
dull and lonely situation, but a short time will in general restore him to his wonted spirits.

Cleanliness, good seed and fresh water, frequently
renewed, are all that are required for a bird in good
health. Green food is not absolutely indispensable
for a bird kept merely for song. It however may
always be given to them as a luxury, and in spring it
operates as a medicine. It cleanses the bowels, cools
and purifies the blood, and a leaf of lettuce or a sprig
of water-cress may be at once useful and ornamental
on the top of the cage. A plentiful supply of green
food should be allowed them in the breeding season,
but unless *chickweed* is quite ripe, it does them more
harm than good. A stick of good ripe seedy plantain is an excellent thing for them in autumn, but it
should not be given to them if green, and all the un-
dergrown part should be thrown away.

Surfeit is the most serious malady with which canaries are affected. It is principally occasioned either by cold or improper diet. It is frequently to be
met with in a whole nest, owing to the young ones
having been furnished with bad food, such as a bad

egg chopped up, dead stale greens left at the bottom of the cage, overgrown coarse unblown chickweed, and putrid water in the glasses.

There are two symptoms of this distemper, exhibited as arising either from cold or overfeeding. In the first case, if, when blowing up the feathers of the belly, it appears swelled, transparent, and full of little red veins, together with the bowels sinking down to its extreme parts, it may be inferred that the bird is in a bad state. In this case the state of the bowels should be carefully attended to. If they are not loose, some gritts should be given in the seed, and a blade of saffron in the water, or as much magnesia as will cover a sixpence, dissolved in the water, for two or three mornings, and a little bread and milk, with a sprinkling of maw seed upon it. If he should be very relaxed, give him, instead of gritts or oatmeal, a little bruised hemp seed and maw seed, which are more binding, and a little dried sponge biscuit, soaked in white wine. When the surfeit seizes your birds in the nest, it is then incurable. This evil may be prevented by a little attention; always considering that as birds have not miles to fly in quest of their food, they have not that air and exercise to carry off the foul humors which overfeeding, carelessness, and colds produce; and they are generally young birds that are affected in this manner.

In birds one, two, or three years old, surfeit is sometimes also produced by too much gross feeding, greens out of season, bad water, and want of gravel at the bottom of the cage. At this age, the disease comes out in scabs, and humors about the head, bill,

11

and eyes, and the running of the humor is so sharp and hot, that it will take the feathers off wherever it spreads over the bodies, and even affect the eyes to blindness.   To cure and stop this, put the bird immediately upon a cooling, purging diet; take away all the canary seed, and let him have only rape seed with some gritts bruised among it, which will cool and scour him out; afterwards anoint the head, or the parts where the feathers have come off, with fresh good hog's lard, or the oil of sweet almonds, two or three times before roosting time.   This treatment will check the disorder. Keep the bird upon this diet until he is purged well, which will make him thin and lean; and when you have conquered the malady, return to the rape and canary mixed; but such is the virulence of the disease, if it attack the eyes, or settle there, in most cases, the sight cannot be saved.   Some persons recommend a strong solution of salt and water, to wash the head and parts where the feathers have come off.   After you have cured your birds, they will look rough and most miserable in feather till they have passed the moulting season.

The *husk* is produced by cold.   It is similar in birds to a dry husky cough, constantly troubling them, and when once caught is not easily cured; therefore strict attention, and that immediately, is necessary ; keep the birds in a warm room, and give them some linseed with their rape and canary for some time, and for a few mornings a small quantity of boiled milk and bread, with maw seed sprinkled over it.— Fresh water every day is indispensable, and a little sugar candy dissolved in it, or a piece of sponge biscuit soaked in white or canary wine, is found to have the happiest effects. These means, with a little care and attention, are all that can be employed with any prospect of successful result. In buying birds, care should be taken that they are not tainted with this malady; and in bringing them home, they should not be hung up where they are exposed to any draught of air; in such a situation, it is very apt to be brought on.

Excessive *perspiration* is a disease that arises from various causes, of which weakness is the principal. It is an almost insuperable concomitant if the hen has been weakly bred; but it also frequently arises from the close and confined situation of the breeding cage, over-heat, a warm season, anxiety and excessive care, with too close sitting upon the eggs or young; all have a tendency to bring it on. If it arises from the latter cause, little can be done, as in attempting to remedy one evil another may be created. In using endeavors to induce her to leave her nest, she may be led to forsake her young. Both time and policy are required in the invention and employment of many little artifices, to wile her away from her pleasing but perilous task. In her situation air and exercise are indispensable requisites, and to entice her off the nest, the cock should be removed for a few days, and hung up in her sight at a short distance; she should be supplied with abundance of green food, to tempt her off the young ones for the purpose of feeding them: and in consequence she will have the privilege of air and exercise in the performance of her duty. When she appears duly occupied with maternal cares, her mate may be restored; and

even although she should not, he must be restored for
the sake of feeding the young.

Weakness may at once be inferred, when it is exhibited by the symptoms of damp and ruffled feathers
before the hen has had eggs or young ones. It is not
advisable to breed with birds of this kind. To cure
this malady, in these circumstances, the bird is sometimes washed with a solution of salt and water for
several mornings, the breeding cage is removed to a
more airy situation, all draughts again are avoided,
and a few drops of sherry are at other times sprinkled over them in the morning; after which they
are set in the sun to dry.

It is doubted much whether any such thing as the
pip exists, from the wren to the goose. A small projection on the rump is found, which some writers tell
us nature has given them, furnished with an oily substance, to trim and keep their feathers in glossy order. Many persons, on seeing this natural promi-
nency, think immediately the bird has got the pip,
when with a pin they hastily make an incision in the
projection, and force out all that which is of service
to the birds; and through this received error, many
a fine bird has been killed. If you should at any
time perceive an extra bladder of matter forming
round or close by the original spot, then you may
prick that inflamed part with a fine needle, and put
on it one drop of the oil of almonds or fresh salad
oil. The true cause of this appearance is, sometimes
your bird will be out of health, set bunchy and twitch
in his tail frequently; when that is the case, see if
his motions be hard, and if so, give him some oatmeal

bruised, and a sprig of water cress for a few mornings to cool and open the body ; change his seed for a few days, and put one or two drops of the spirit of nitre into his fresh water for two or three mornings ; some persons will recommend a feather or two to be pulled out of the tail, but I do not ; only draw a tail feather or two, in case of a fit, or dropping down apparently dead, as that will fetch blood, and sometimes recover the bird.

The complaint of *egg-bound* proceeds from cold, and especially the coldness of the spring weather, which is so very uncertain in this country ; therefore, it is best not to put your birds up too early, but to wait till the weather is settled a little : the last week of the March month is generally early enough to put them into the breeding cage. Cold weather likewise causes the birds to have soft eggs, that is, no hard shell when laid. Therefore, begin not too early, especially as a room without any fire is the best ; give the bird a little moist sugar with the bread and egg, which will cause a slipperiness and openness for the egg. Should the hen be very bad, and scarcely able to move, or if she is down in a bunch at the bottom of the cage, take her gently out with a warm hand, and anoint the abdominal part with two or three drops of warm salad oil, or the oil of almonds. By this she will generally be relieved, and the egg will be found laid or dropped about the cage in the course of a few hours, or, at the farthest, by next morning. With a maiden hen this frequently happens, and if the above means fail, the last resource is, to pour down her throat, through a reed or quill, one drop of castor oil.

Moulting sometimes exhibits a diseased type.—
Birds bred up in the manner we have directed, in a
good and healthy air, as near as possible to a state of
nature, moult off strong, clean, and without any assistance, but at times even the best require attention.
Cold is the greatest danger to which in this state
they are exposed, therefore all draughts of air should
be carefully guarded against.

In itself it cannot be prevented, and when it happens in the due course of nature it should be encouraged rather than checked. Nature has, however, no
object to borrow at times the helping hand of man to
assist her feathered offspring in throwing off their
glossy coats. The top and sides of the cage may be
covered up with paper to keep the birds warm, and
the cleaning of the cage may be omitted for two or
three weeks. A little saffron in their water, a little
nourishing bread, egg, or maw seed, will speedily
clothe the birds in a plumage more beautiful than that
in which they were.

The covering of the cage should not be taken off
all at once, but gradually ; it should then be cleaned
thoroughly, and the birds fed as usual. Fresh water
should be given to them every day plentifully, and
they should be put in the sun for an hour or two if
the weather is fine, when they will be seen assisting
nature by plucking off their feathers.

The first moult, which takes place when they are
about three months old, is partial. The birds then
throw off all their down and loose feathers, and produce their full blooming plumage. The moult of September is the general time of moulting for old birds.

All the young birds are put by the fancy canary amateurs and prize competitors in the stock cage, to produce a premature moult and silken plumage. In this there may be policy, but great imprudence, as from his removal from a glazed cage to an open one the bird is apt to catch cold, and from the mere change of temperature to droop and die. The hand that receives the prize at a canary show is often doomed the same day to consign the successful competitor to the tomb—all arising from this stock-cage nursing. The tail and wing feathers are changed by all finches in the second year's moulting. On this account, those parts become lighter and brighter every year, and a fancy canary can even compete for a prize beyond his first twelvemonth. Some birds are more nervous than other; and sudden bustle or noise near the cage will frighten one, while not the slightest effect is produced upon another. If a bird has dropped down in a fit without any apparent cause, some connoisseurs pull a feather or two out of the tail, or instantly plunge the bird into cold water. He is then restored to the cage and induced by every means to drink, and if he can be brought to take a single drop, he immediately recovers. After this, a drop of the spirits of nitre should be put into his water-glass for two or three mornings. Sometimes a canary will drop down by exhausting his strength, from singing in rivalry with another. In this case he should be recovered by the most gentle means, and the greatest good may be done by getting the smallest quantity of canary wine into his bill; some persons try to recover the goldfinch, when in a fit, by cutting the tip of the under claw, washing the legs in white wine, and giving a drop of wine in sugar to moisten the bill.— If birds have repeated fits, nothing better can be done than giving them frequently a little nitre in the water that they drink.